COURTS AND RIGHTS

The American Judiciary in Action

STUDIES IN
POLITICAL
SCIENCE

COURTS AND RIGHTS

The American Judiciary in Action

By

JOHN P. ROCHE

Brandeis University

RANDOM HOUSE
New York

TO
THE MEMORY OF WALTER JOHN ROCHE
1888—1958
AND
THE DREAMS OF JOANNA
RATCLIFF ROCHE
1955—

PREFACE

This book, while undeniably the work of the author, is also an acknowledgment of indebtedness to many. I have been fortunate in my friends—and friendly opponents—who have supplied me with that most priceless of all scholarly gifts: frank unsparing criticism. Naturally enough, I have often writhed under the lash, but one can learn nothing from academic courtiers.

Foremost in the ranks of dedicated critics has been my friend Leonard W. Levy, that flinty-eyed master of constitutional microanalysis and ascorbic enemy of "poetic" generalizations. Others to whom I owe long-standing obligations for the contributions they have made to my analytical framework are Edmond N. Cahn, Robert E. Cushman, David Fellman, Howard Jay Graham, Clinton Rossiter, and Milton Sacks. But while they may be in loco parentis, I trust no one will lodge any paternity suits: I suspect at least three of these friends would disagree vigorously with my general position on judicial review.

Finally, my wife Constance must be thanked for devoting much of her time to frustrating the guileful efforts of our daughter Joanna to convince me that writing is a waste of time that could more profitably be employed playing with her.

J. P. R.
Waltham, Mass.
April, 1961

CONTENTS

- I -

THE RULE OF LAW

In the summer of 1957, there gathered at Runnymede in England a distinguished group of American lawyers and judges including the Chief Justice of the United States, Earl Warren. In the presence of some rather puzzled and slightly amused Englishmen, these visitors dedicated a monument to *Magna Carta* in the field where in 1215 King John capitulated to the baronage. The oratory which accompanied the ceremony emphasized one theme over and over again: the vital significance of the Great Charter in the growth of the rule of law. Although some snide British dons observed what a shame it was the Americans had no home-grown monuments to the rule of law, and English antiquarians scurried to point out that the Charter was in essence a reactionary feudal document, this ingenuous gesture symbolized the deep American sense of indebtedness to the British legal tradition. And if the original *Magna Carta* was something less than a passionate blow for liberty, it is nonetheless the case that the myth of *Magna Carta* as a subordination of the King to Law has over the centuries achieved an autonomous existence. When in 1628 Sir Edward Coke rose in the House of Commons to declare that "Magna Charta is such a fellow, that he will have no 'Sovereign,'" he was stretching historical fact a bit, but this polemical exaggeration became a potent weapon in the struggle for justice.

This volume is concerned with the struggle for justice

in the United States, specifically with the judicial aspects of that struggle. But before launching an intensive inquiry into the organization of federal judicial power and the operation of this power in the crucial area of civil rights, it is essential briefly to describe the context, both jurisprudential and institutional, within which judicial activity occurs.

At the outset we must spend some time in historical analysis examining the development of the concept of the "rule of law." The fundamental proposition can be traced to antiquity; it is found in both Plato and Aristotle as the foundation of the "second-best" *polis,* the best being rule by a "philosopher-king." In Book III of the *Politics,* Aristotle provided the classic definition of law as rule by "God and reason alone" or "reason free from all passion." This definition, which emphasizes the impersonal, disembodied character of law as distinct from the self-interested command of a king or community, has echoed down through the intervening centuries. It can be found, in a formulation borrowed from the seventeenth-century English theorist James Harrington (a favorite of John Adams), in the Massachusetts Constitution of 1780: "a Government of Laws and not of Men." [1]

With the rise of Christianity, law was given a new rationale, but the essential formulation remained the same. The Christian God became the source of law; the Holy Roman and Apostolic Church was the authoritative interpretative agency, but law itself was seen as a set of eternal transcendent principles which operated impersonally on mankind. When John of Salisbury in the eleventh century argued that a lawless tyrant could legitimately be destroyed, it did not seem to enter his mind that a human decision was involved in the process. To the criticism that in fact the Church, a body of human beings, was determining a king's action to be violative of God's laws, Salisbury would presumably have replied that these churchmen did not *make* decisions, they only ascertained God's will, a wholly impersonal process analogous to measuring rainfall.[2]

Two centuries later, St. Thomas Aquinas gave to the medieval world his classic formulation of Christian Aristotelianism. Far more subtle than John of Salisbury, St. Thomas tended to hedge his theoretical bets with prudential considerations. For example, like John he condemned lawless tyranny, but he distinguished two categories of tyrant (one by essence and one by will) and reserved his most vigorous strictures for those who "snatched power by violence." "Every law," St. Thomas stated, "is ordered to the common good, and a precept has the force of law only when it serves this community benefit." However, it was perfectly clear that St. Thomas felt all law had its ultimate foundation in eternal law, the mind of God, and that any contrary enactment was void. On the crucial question of who had the power to define law and distinguish it from no-law, the great Dominican was ambiguous. Unlike Salisbury, he was no militant papalist—indeed, he hardly touched upon the sticky issue of the relationship between *imperium* and *sacerdotium,* secular and religious spheres of authority—and one can only emerge with a tentative conclusion that reason was the measuring rod and the community-as-a-whole the body with jurisdiction.[3]

Law is a great deal more than theory, but before we examine its institutional character it is important to emphasize that all were agreed that law was not a human artifact. A few dissenting voices were registered, notably the Sophists who were the end-men in Plato's dialogues, but their views were either suppressed or forgotten.[4] It was accepted that there was a law of nature (the Stoic-Roman view) or an eternal law (the Christian formulation) which existed independently of human perception or action and which served as a yardstick for measuring the legitimacy of civil or man-made law. Even those, like St. Augustine, who took a dim view of man's ability to fulfill divine ordinances and took for granted the corrupt status of mundane institutions, accepted the existence of this order of righteousness, this transcendent standard of virtue.

To look at the matter from a different perspective, that

of élite theory, it was generally conceded that the power of a king or aristocracy was no criterion of legitimacy. Rather, the authority of rulers was derived from their position in law. This was not a contradiction to the view that kingship had a divine origin, the doctrine of the divine right of kings, except in the latter's extreme Eastern form. We must never forget that primitive societies are far more complex juridically than advanced communities; a great deal of what has been written about the divine right of kings implies that medieval legists and political philosophers were simple-minded boobs when in fact the opposite was the case. They operated easily with a set of the most intricate theoretical propositions. Both the Roman jurisconsuls and medieval civilians (experts in the Roman or civil law) would laugh scornfully at the naïveté of their critics. Those who esteem highly "that Divinity that doth hedge a King" are advised to recall the source and read with care Shakespeare's narrative of the "un-kinging" of Richard II *in the name of the Crown*.[5]

We might examine two aspects of the divine right of kings to get the flavor of the exegesis that, in theory at least, domesticated absolutism. The great Roman lawyers viewed the doctrine of the emperor's divinity, proclaimed by Caesar Augustus, as a fiction which was extremely useful in impressing Eastern peasants. As far as Roman law was concerned, it was utterly irrelevant; indeed, long after the emperors had become absolute despots the lawyers were arguing that their absolute authority was a delegation from the Roman people, that the *lex regia* conferred dictatorial powers! In the sixth century Justinian's Code—a massive systematization and collation of the Roman law—expressed the view that the provisions were a detailed elaboration of the principles of natural justice. In short, the Code defined Roman justice; but justice was not just that which the Code defined, it was a set of anterior principles.[6]

The Christian theorists had a problem of their own occasioned by St. Paul's *Epistle to the Romans* (xiii). "Let every person be subject to the governing authorities," instructed the apostle, "for there is no authority except from God, and those that exist have been instituted by God. Therefore he who resists the authorities resists what God has appointed. . . ." On its face this was a strong statement of the divine inspiration of rulership, even of tyranny, but the process of rationalistic erosion began early; in the fifth century, Cassiodorus pointed out that properly interpreted the text meant "let every person be subject to *just* rulers, for there is no *just* authority but from God." [7] In essence Cassiodorus reified kingship, *i.e.,* treated the abstraction as a thing, so that one could make the distinction between just authority (from God) and a bad ruler. Thus God had ordained the *principle* of just rule, not the *persons* of wicked or heretical kings. Even the most sophisticated modern dialectician must concede the finesse involved in this gloss. Later St. Thomas picked up the same theme in his *Commentary on the Sentences of Peter Lombard* and gave the formulation its lasting polish.[8]

Modern commentators, particularly those who feel that in our time the masses have gotten out of hand, are fond of pointing nostalgically to the Middle Ages as an "Age of Faith" where community was built around convictions and clerks were treated with the deference they merit. As the example above suggests, nothing could be more naive. While medieval theorists believed abstractly in the divine right of kings and could quote St. Paul in Latin (*"Qui potestati resistit, Dei ordinationi resistit."*), the consequences of belief were open-ended: one could as easily in good faith kill a king as defend one. The doubter is referred to the history of the Byzantine Empire where the "divine emperors" required from their subjects *proskynesis* (full prostration), presumably to reduce the risk of assassination!

But whatever may have been the political reality—and it was pretty dreadful—the important consideration for our purposes was the maintenance of the *myth of limitation,* the ideal cherished by the Roman and Christian commentators that earthly power was exercised within, and obtained its jurisdiction from, a framework of eternal principles. Like the myth of *Magna Carta* referred to earlier, this conception of a higher-law referent was later to play an important role in justifying those natural rights which Englishmen of the seventeenth century and Americans of the eighteenth so vigorously asserted.

The fifteenth and sixteenth centuries saw the emergence of the concept of sovereignty, *i.e.,* the view that final authority resided in the sovereign and that the postulation of an external standard was effectively treason. In immediate terms, this was the secular equivalent of the Reformation, designed to check the temporal power of the Church as the Protestants aimed to check its spiritual jurisdiction. The Reformation was, as Sheldon Wolin has shown in his fine study *Politics and Vision*[9] and as R. H. Tawney suggested many years ago in a different context,[10] a highly differentiated phenomenon. Without venturing into the complex ecclesiastical polities of Calvin, Luther, or the Anabaptists, it is safe to say that they all took a low view of temporal rulers, at least in functional terms. However, in historical impact Calvinism was radically different from Lutheranism; whereas Lutherans took refuge from legal problems in other-worldly concerns—thus vacating the realm of public morality—the Calvinists became militant spokesmen of a Divine Law higher than princes.[11]

In pragmatic terms, one can make the case that the Calvinists' concern for higher law was a direct function of their inability in most places to control lower law. When the Catholics and the Lutherans made their great division of Germany at the Peace of Augsburg in 1555, for example, both participants formed a united front against the recognition of Calvinism ("The Calvinist dragon," a Lutheran spokesman noted charitably, "is pregnant with all the horrors of Mohammedanism").[12] And in France the Huguenot assault against royal despotism which achieved its apotheosis in the *Vindication of Liberty Against Tyrants* (1577) quietly petered out when Henry IV, a Protestant convert to Catholicism accused by the Jesuits of fake conversion, took the throne.[13] But however motivated, the Calvinists did in most situations fight bitterly against the principle of sovereignty—and like the Communists, whom they resembled in many organizational ways, they were capable of raising a terrific furor.

The basic pattern of religious settlement—in England, the Germanies, and even in Catholic states like France and Spain—was an affirmation of the principle of sovereignty. In England and the Germanies it was overt: Henry VIII nationalized the Church and set himself as its head, while the Peace of Augsburg supplied Germany with the classic formula *cujus regio ejus religio,* the religion of the people would be that of the prince—whether he were Lutheran or Catholic. The secular authority was in this fashion given final control over the faith of the populace. The voice of the sovereign became the voice of God and the fundamental political and legal ideals of fifteen hundred years crumbled to ashes. In Catholic countries, the sovereign assumed similar authority without benefit of clergy: the Church was subordinated to the state and the ties with Rome became largely ceremonial in nature.

The practice of sovereignty had by this time far outrun the theory. Late medieval commentators such as Marsilius of Padua, Jean Bodin, and Niccolò Machiavelli were groping for the appropriate formulation, but they all—even Machiavelli—were to some degree prisoners of the antique ideology and were thus incapable of flatly stating, "Law is the command of the sovereign." Always in their writings there are vague concepts of limitation fluttering in the background somewhere, limitations which *ought* to operate even if in practical terms they appeared evanescent. It remained for that towering seventeenth-century figure, half genius, half crackpot, Thomas Hobbes to lay the cards on the table.

Much time and metaphysical effort has gone into disputes over whether Thomas Hobbes believed in higher law or in God. I find this discussion analytically meaningless; if Hobbes believed in God in any theistic sense, which I doubt, it would not have altered his axioms in the slightest. The only higher law he accepted was Newtonian: human behavior is founded on certain laws of mass and motion with

self-preservation as the one key postulate. In institutional
terms, he made it clear that for the citizen law was, and was
only, "those Rules which the Commonwealth hath com-
manded him by Word, Writing, or other sufficient Sign of
the Will, to make use of for the Distinction of Right and
Wrong." Law, in short, was a "Command" of the sovereign—no more, no less. And he inveighed sardonically
against those who would invoke the "Ghostly Power" of
religion as a standard of judgment for the laws of the
commonwealth. The only natural right the individual pos-
sessed was that of self-defense against the threat of
destruction and this was premised on egoistic atomism: if
a little rock had a mind, it would not permit itself to be
placed in the path of a big rock—and similarly with man,
who *is* a rock with a mind.

Hobbes, in other words, declared unambiguously that
there are no checks on the power of the sovereign. Law
is the command of the king or Parliament—Hobbes' "sovereign" being a legal "person" in the same sense that corporations are legal "persons." The Sage of Malmesbury, who
was a decent soul, *hoped* that sovereigns would abide by
certain moral propositions, but his genial hopes were
completely without institutional support. There was no
basis for appealing a decision of the sovereign except self-
defense; in Hobbes' system it was *ex hypothese* impossible
to declare a law unconstitutional, unjust, or void. The
laws were the only criterion of justice.[14]

Later in the seventeenth century John Locke added a
new dimension to Hobbes' system. Locke, in my reading,
accepted the Hobbesian concept of sovereignty intact but
added several necessary preconditions for its existence,
primarily the representative character of the sovereign
legislature. The cutting edge of his views in the *Second
Treatise* was directed at arbitrary, capricious *executive*
authority: he believed that in regard to domestic affairs
the executive was no more than the agent of the legislature.
Thus a citizen who had been deprived of his property rights,
which Locke defined broadly as "life, liberty, and estate,"
by the executive without legislative sanction had recourse

to revolution. (Perhaps Locke was thinking of royal efforts to tax the people, as Charles I had attempted in Ship Money, without Parliamentary agreement?) The individual also had rights against an unrepresentative legislature. (Perhaps Locke was here thinking of another seventeenth-century British event, the purged or "Rump" Parliament of 1648?) However, if the citizen did not like the decisions of a representative Parliament—and Locke in Sec. 119 of the *Second Treatise* defined representation very broadly —his only alternatives were to submit or emigrate.[15]

Yet while Locke normally accepted the acts of the sovereign as final and unappealable, his general theory in the context of the eighteenth century supplied the rationale for a new assertion of higher law, natural rights doctrine. A careless reading of Locke's *Second Treatise* suggests that he was a militant defender of the rights of the citizen against government in general—just as a sloppy appraisal of his *Letter Concerning Toleration* converts him into a libertarian ("no opinions contrary to human society, or to those moral rules which are necessary to the preservation of civil society, are to be tolerated," "those are not at all to be tolerated who deny the being of a God.").[16] But, while those who read Locke in this favorable fashion deserved no more than C— in Political Theory, this version had an enormous impact, particularly in the American colonies. John Locke by one of history's little ironies became the patron saint of those Americans who set out to undermine the authority of Locke's omnipotent Parliament!

From 1761 on, colonial leaders were invoking "natural rights" as a bar to British encroachments on local authority. Working within the Lockian framework, they initially challenged Parliamentary power on the grounds of non-representation: "No taxation without Representation." This position was difficult to maintain in the face of the British reply that geography was not the real basis of Parliamentary representation, that in fact several of England's larger cities were without Members of Parliament, that according to the theory of "virtual representation" every Member was a representative of the common interest of Englishmen everywhere, not just of his district. Without exploring the intervening stages in the argument, the doctrine of "inalienable rights" was finally in the Declaration of Independence based on a remarkable inversion of Lockian ideas. The authors of the Declaration accused the king of breaking the social contract and proceeded to denounce George III in terms appropriate only to a Tudor despot; Parliament was given two passing references, both to the effect that the king had cheated by authorizing the legislature to enact rules for the colonies.[17]

To say this, as the authors must have known (they were first-class political scientists), was to stand British eighteenth-century history on its head. King and Parliament were inextricably bound together by 1776 as a consequence of the great Whig heritage, and it was the King-in-Parliament which had enacted laws which the colonists found oppressive.[18] But the argument of the Declaration, one of the world's great masterpieces of political warfare, adjusted the facts to fit the Lockian model of a usurping monarch, ignored Locke's sovereign legislature, and invoked the right of revolution. The higher-law concept of political legitimacy returned to politics with a vengeance.

As soon as the colonists achieved *de facto* sovereignty, they promptly put Locke back on his feet and became vigorous advocates of legislative determination of natural law and ruthless oppressors of the Tory minority which had evinced a sudden interest in its natural rights against the natural righters.[19] One hesitates to be cynical about this sort of thing, but perhaps there is a fundamental philosophical truth in the observation of that frontier sage Bret Maverick: "The dealer always cheats." Yet, however much chicanery may have been involved in defining natural rights, it is again important to emphasize that the Americans restored the myth to its ancient position, reclaiming the ideal of the rule of law from the empiricist clutches of Hobbes and his followers.

The American Constitution in effect buried the Hobbesian concept of sovereignty under an intricate system of checks and balances. This was not the result of following some blueprint of "federalism"—federalism was a set of *ad hoc* arrangements which were later elevated into a political theory—but rather of compromise between those defending the powers of the states and those who demanded sovereignty for the new general government. But the outcome was an elaborate set of roadblocks to tyranny, even to efficient nontyrannical action. The power of final decision was so hedged about that, at least in theory, a high level of consensus was required before significant action could be taken. Within the national government itself, powers were merged, not separated, so that the executive, legislative, and judicial branches all had checks on each other (the President's veto, for example, gives him the same amount of legislative power as two-thirds of Congress). And the suspicious states, fearful of this new "engine of oppression," demanded in the Bill of Rights still further guarantees.

While the Constitution and Bill of Rights did little to protect the individual citizen—indeed, the Bill of Rights enforced standards of legal procedure on the federal government that were observed in few states[20]—the system which developed assumed limitation of power on all sides. By the time proposed enactments had been filtered through the convoluted pipes and fine screens, they would be impersonalized and deprived of any arbitrary or capricious characteristics.[21] The consequence would be the rule of law, a government of laws and not of men. It would be a polity in which all decisions or statutes could be measured against the words of a written Constitution—the rule of law incarnate.

This, then, was the ideal as it finally emerged in America and became part of American constitutionalism. But the rule of law is more than an abstraction and we must now turn to the history of judicial institutions to discover by what techniques the dream of impartial justice was little by little given institutional meaning. In short, we must move from an examination of the rule of law to one of the rule of lawyers.

- 2 -

THE JUDICIAL PROCESS

To anyone accustomed to the orderly centralization of the French or British judicial systems, the American arrangement presents an intricate and confusing pattern. Instead of one national structure, there are in the United States fifty-one discrete systems; instead of one body of law of universal application, there are fifty-one legal codes. Each state has and exercises its sovereign right to establish both norms of judicial procedure and canons of legal decision, subject only to generalized restraints imposed by the Supremacy Clause of the Constitution (Article VI) and the injunctions of Section 1 of the Fourteenth Amendment.

Varying state techniques often betray the variety of juridical ancestors which once populated the land. Louisiana, for example, has active remnants of French law; California and the other states of the Old Spanish settlement retain traces of Spanish precedents. But in every case, these have been overlaid by the Anglo-American legal tradition which accompanied the settlers first on their great transatlantic emigration and then on their march to the Pacific. The American Revolution repudiated the Crown as the ultimate source of law, but retained the King's law virtually intact. As the Virginia Convention of 1776 put it, "the common law of England, all statutes or acts of parliament made in aid of the common law prior to the fourth year of the reign of King James the first

(1607), and which are of a general nature, not local to that kingdom . . . shall be the rule of decision, and shall be considered as in full force, until the same shall be altered by the legislative power of this colony." [1] Each state made its own modifications, but the essence of English law remained as the foundation of American jurisprudence.

In examining national judicial institutions a discussion of the state legal systems may seem irrelevant. Unfortunately from the viewpoint of the student and the lawyer who practices in the federal courts it is not. While the national government has its own distinct set of courts ranging from the District courts at the bottom of the pyramid through the Courts of Appeal to the Supreme Court at the apex, and federal jurisdiction also has its own immense criminal and civil codes, federal judges must perpetually take cognizance of state laws, and even of state judicial decisions. State and federal authority intermesh at many points: federal judges must apply state law to a certain category of cases, state courts on occasion fulfill federal functions, such as naturalization of aliens, and of course any state court of appropriate jurisdiction can declare a national statute unconstitutional or the act of a federal officer illegal. Some of these intricacies will be elaborated in the subsequent discussion of the jurisdiction of the federal courts. First, however, some history is in order so the student can get some perspective on the development of the federal judicial structure.

The Structure of the Federal Judiciary

At the time the Constitution was drawn up, there was considerable difference of opinion among the delegates to the Convention on whether the new general government should have a full judicial system of its own. Some of the framers, notably those associated with the Paterson, or New Jersey, Plan, felt that the federal government could utilize state courts for its business, retaining only its own supreme court to oversee the decisions below. Characteristically, the authors of the Constitution ducked the issue by recourse to ambiguity, leaving final settlement of the problem to the future. Article III of the Constitution merely provided that there was to be "one Supreme Court, and such inferior Courts as the Congress may from time to time ordain and establish." [2]

Once the new government got under way, immediate action was initiated to establish a separate system of national courts. Senate Bill No. 1 in the First Congress was an act to establish a federal judiciary; significantly, the Committee which drafted the measure was chaired by Oliver Ellsworth and included two other former delegates to the Federal Convention. The Judiciary Act of 1789 established the structure of the federal courts as rigorously distinct from state judiciaries, and indeed set a judicial pattern which lasted without significant alteration until 1891. Moreover, in Section 25, this act firmly superimposed the constitutional authority of the Supreme Court of the United States upon the state courts.

As compared with our symmetrical national judicial structure today, the court system established by the Judiciary Act of 1789 was confusing and unsymmetrical. The Supreme Court was given a membership of six; the Chief Justice and five Associate Justices. Below the Supreme Court were two categories of inferior tribunals, the District and the Circuit courts. The country was divided into thirteen districts, each state constituting a district except Virginia and Massachusetts which were divided into two districts (Rhode Island and North Carolina were not yet in the Union). Three Circuits were simultaneously set up, each encompassing roughly a third of the nation. There were, however, only two sets of judges: District judges, one for each district, and Supreme Court judges. A Circuit Court consisted of two justices of the Supreme Court and the judge of the district in which the Circuit Court, which traveled from district to district, was sitting.

The jurisdiction of the District and Circuit courts was functionally determined, that is, the District courts were largely concerned with admiralty and maritime cases, while the Circuit courts handled mostly cases arising between citizens of different states. Under the Constitution, the federal courts have two sources of jurisdiction: diversity of citizenship, or suits between citizens of different states, and federal questions, or suits which are based on the Constitution and laws of the United States. In the first sort of case, which was then made the responsibility of the Circuit courts, it is the character of the litigants which vests jurisdiction in the federal judiciary; in the second, it is the character of the subject matter which brings the matter before the federal forum, and these cases were generally assigned to the District courts. In a very small number of instances it was possible to appeal from a District to a Circuit Court, but effectively both types of court were vested with original jurisdiction, *i.e.,* they were in legal parlance courts of first instance or *nisi prius* courts. Normally appeals from both were lodged with the Supreme Court.[3]

The Supreme Court which met in New York in 1790 was in one important sense comparable to our Court today —its justices were politicians primarily, and only in an ancillary sense legalists. All had been active supporters of the Constitution: Wilson, Rutledge, and Blair had been at the Convention; John Jay was a contributor to the *Federalist* papers; and Iredell and Cushing had been strong spokesmen for ratification in their respective states. There had been no shortage of candidates for the high Court positions. James Wilson, for example, offered to sacrifice himself on the altar of duty in a letter to President Washington which merits partial quotation:

"I commit myself to your Excellency without reserve and inform you that my aim rises to the important office of Chief Justice of the United States. But how shall I proceed? Shall I enumerate reasons in justification of my high pretensions? I have not yet employed my pen in my own praise. When I make those high pretensions and offer them to so good a judge, can I say that they are altogether without foundation? Your Excellency must relieve me from this dilemma." [4]

Though Wilson was probably the ablest legal mind in the country, Washington could not risk making such a notorious land speculator Chief Justice, but he did make him one of the Associate Justices. The President's caution was justified by events: poor Wilson, still a Justice, died a pauper's death in hiding from his creditors.[5]

For the Supreme Court to exist was one thing; for it to exercise and define its authority was something else. Throughout the first decade of the Republic, the Court exerted little authority. Indeed, in only one instance did it really go out on a limb—when it held that sovereign states were liable to suit by individual citizens of other states (*Chisholm* v. *Georgia,* 1793)—and this limb was hastily sawed off by the Eleventh Amendment to the Constitution. The extent of judicial power remained vague and unresolved.

Judicial Review

From the very outset, judges in America, both on the state and on the national level, were far more than technicians, far more than merely legal experts charged with interpreting the meaning of statutes and ordinances. The concept of checks and balances, the perpetual quest for equilibrium which suffused American constitutionalism must be recalled here. Suffice it to note that the principle of equilibrium required that judges be more than puppets of a legislature. In the constitutional scheme of things, it was imperative that some institution exist to protect the very fabric of the Constitution, to insure that a legislature and an executive would not connive together to break the equilibrium of forces. Moreover, the intricate meshing of state and national authorities in the American Constitution required an agency to enforce the Supremacy Clause upon the states, to see to it that the acts of these coordinate yet subordinate sovereignties did not violate

the Constitution, the laws, and the treaties of the United
States.

Some have denied that the framers of the Constitution
could have intended to give the power to overrule Congress
to the Supreme Court on the ground that this would have
given the Court final power—and the framers never gave
any institution "final power." This view is founded on
a misreading of history, for there was a counter to judicial
action in the power to amend the Constitution. In fact, as
was noted above, the Court's first venture into controversy
brought an immediate amendment to curb its presumed
jurisdiction. In this connection it must be recalled that to
the framers, the states were the main threat to the bonds
of Union and the Court's check on the states was in turn
balanced by the power of amendment at a time when the
Senate directly represented state interests. (Senators were
"instructed" by their state legislatures on important policies
and were expected to resign if they would not accept in-
struction.) Thus if two-thirds of the House and Senate
voted an amendment, it was likely to reflect the viewpoint
of an overwhelming proportion of the state legislatures.
If we are to believe Hamilton's explicit statement in the
Federalist (No. 78) (one must be very careful to recall
that the *Federalist* papers were propaganda for the Constitution, not an authoritative gloss on its meaning), the
Supreme Court was also expected to keep the national
legislature within the constitutional paddock.

Though the arguments for judicial review of state and of
national action are theoretically identical, the two aspects
must be separated for analytical purposes. For one thing,
the right to oversee state action has been far more frequently and effectively employed, and secondly, such
power was explicitly given to the Supreme Court by Section 25 of the Judiciary Act of 1789. That Act provided:

"That a final judgment or decree in any suit, in the highest
court of law or equity of a State . . . where is drawn in
question the validity of a treaty or statute of, or an authority
exercised under, the United States, and the decision is

> against their validity; or where is drawn in question the
> validity of a statute of, or an authority exercised under,
> any State, on the ground of their being repugnant to the
> constitution, treaties, or laws of the United States . . . or
> where is drawn in question the construction of any clause
> of the constitution, or of a treaty, or statute of, or com-
> mission held under, the United States . . . may be re-
> examined, and reversed or affirmed in the Supreme Court
> of the United States." [6]

Without getting involved in the legal convolutions necessary properly to interpret this text, it can be stated that
it supplied the Court with a weapon adequate for its needs.
Despite some fulminations by states'-righters, and several
efforts to repeal this provision, the authority remained
and, as we shall see, was vigorously exercised in several
pathbreaking decisions by the Marshall Court.

The power to declare acts of Congress unconstitutional,
while inherent in constitutional theory, was nowhere set
forth in clear terms. As is customary today, the statesmen
of the federal period took the inconsistent view that the
Court should declare unconstitutional those acts of Congress which they deplored and called judicial decisions
which went against their vested interests "unconstitutional
usurpations." For example, the same Jeffersonians who
denounced John Marshall's holding Section 13 of the
Judiciary Act of 1789 unconstitutional (*Marbury* v. *Madison*, 1803) had distinguished themselves in the Adams
administration by their demands that the high Court
declare the Alien and Sedition Acts unconstitutional and
void.[7]

Marbury v. *Madison* deserves extended examination as
a classic instance of judicial legerdemain. In purely legal
terms, the decision was contrived and absurd, but it was
a masterpiece of political chicanery. Without going too
deeply into the details (among other weird events, the
United States Attorney General under questioning by
Chief Justice Marshall invoked the Fifth Amendment and
refused to testify on the ground that he might incriminate

himself!) it is perhaps fair to say that Marshall's political footwork was as superlative as his legal reasoning was spurious. The net result was that by a patent misinterpretation of Section 13 of the Judiciary Act the Chief Justice found that Congress had violated the Constitution by adding to the constitutionally stipulated original jurisdiction of the Supreme Court.[8] Since Marbury had brought his case under this allegedly unconstitutional proviso, the Court had no jurisdiction and Marbury had to go elsewhere in search of legal redress. However, along the way Marshall managed to make clear his view that Jefferson and Madison had viciously and illegally done in poor Marbury. In short, Marshall employed the Marbury case as a vehicle for giving President Jefferson a lecture on political morality and then announced that unfortunately the Supreme Court could not restore Marbury to his privileges as a justice of the peace of the District of Columbia because the act of Congress which Marbury had relied on for succor was unconstitutional! As the great historian Henry Adams put it with his characteristic irony, "The strongest admirers of Marshall admitted that his manner of dealing with this case was unusual." [9]

President Jefferson was infuriated by Marshall's partisan tract, but the latter was in the happy position of holding a strong defensive line. He had not demanded anything of the President nor had he significantly affronted the Congress —which at this time was thoroughly out of sympathy with the *whole* Judiciary Act of 1789; he had merely limited the power of the Supreme Court. Nevertheless, the Chief Justice *had* exercised the power to declare an act of the national legislature unconstitutional and the precedent was established for future reference.

While it is technically correct to state that this power was not again exercised until the *Dred Scott Case* (1857), it should be added that in the interim the Court many times was asked to declare acts of Congress unconstitutional but rejected the proffered sword. Marshall himself in 1805 (*United States* v. *Fisher*) and in the famous Bank case

(*McCulloch* v. *Maryland,* 1819) sustained as constitutional challenged exercises of national legislative power, and in a significant District Court case (*United States* v. *Brigantine William,* 1808) a judge asserted the constitutionality of Jefferson's Embargo Act, the most far-reaching regulation of national commerce yet known. The irony of this case was that the Jeffersonians were elated by the court's exercise of judicial review, and the Federalists, who had cheered Marshall in 1803, denounced the judge for his usurpation of power. The basic canon of constitutional interpretation has always been "Whose ox is gored?"

The Political Role of the Federal Judiciary

This brings us squarely to grips with the anomalous position of the federal judiciary in the American political system. Federal judges obviously have exercised political functions, yet in the technical sense they are wholly irresponsible, *i.e.,* they are appointed for life and are in no way responsible to the people for their actions. The only checks on judicial actions are latent: the possibility of impeachment, a Congressional decision to limit federal jurisdiction, and the graveyard. Except for a case of clear criminal behavior, impeachment is a dead letter. Thomas Jefferson tried to rid the Supreme Court of Justice Samuel Chase, a malignant Federalist partisan who in 1798-1800 had from his vantage point on the bench poured his venom on Jefferson and his followers as virtual traitors, but failed to muster the necessary two-thirds vote on the Senate to convict. (It was rumored at the time that had the ax fallen on Chase, Marshall was next for the block.) The failure of the action against Chase established the precedent that a judge's political views, no matter how extreme, were unlikely to constitute adequate grounds for a purge.

If judges were, on the British or French model, technicians who applied law to specific cases at bar, this irresponsibility would hardly constitute a problem. In the great bulk of the work of a federal judge, both now and in the past, it must be noted that he *is* essentially a technician. No one, for example, would urge that a District judge's decision in a patent suit should be subject to majority approval before going into effect. The real issue is concerned with a minute proportion of the decisions of the federal courts and notably of the Supreme Court. In this category of decision, the judges move from their role as administrators of legal expertise to a position as political decision-makers. Of course, there is always a legal justification for their assuming this role, but given the open-ended quality of legal principles, it would be a pretty incompetent judge who could not discover legal justification for doing what he wanted to do. As the first Justice John M. Harlan once blandly observed to some law students, "I want to say to you young gentlemen that if we don't like an act of Congress, we don't have much trouble to find grounds for declaring it unconstitutional." [10]

With this freedom of maneuver, judges can invade the arena of political decision-making, and the history of American constitutional law is marked by notorious instances of such intervention. The most recent is, of course, the 1954 and 1955 decisions in the *School Segregation Cases*. Politicians and students can argue almost indefinitely whether this sort of judicial meddling is "democratic" or "undemocratic"—and we shall not examine that fascinating question at this point—but no one versed in history can deny that it is both constitutional and traditional. What is much more important from the viewpoint of the student is the political structure which makes this possible. Why have Americans permitted their judiciary such wide-ranging power? Why have American courts not been subjugated by legislative majorities and denied the right to substitute judicial judgment for the judgment of popularly elected majorities? In short, why has the British pattern of judicial subordination to Parliament not developed in the United States? British judges too are appointed for life, but they confine themselves to legal crocheting and never tamper with the decisions of Parliament.

The answer here seems to be related to the discussion of American political parties. American parties are not strongly organized national instruments, but are composed of coalitions of local party organizations with very tenuous national bonds. Once every four years, the various factions within the Democratic and Republican coalitions bury the hatchet and nominate a candidate for President. Between presidential elections, only the generally bankrupt national committees exist to remind the populace that another election is in the offing and to try to raise money to pay the debts incurred in the last battle. In Congress, party solidarity is maintained at the expense of ideological purity: within the Democratic and Republican congressional delegations there is constant conflict between liberals and conservatives and on legislative issues such as minimum wage extension the liberals in both parties vote together against the rural Republicans and the Southern conservative Democrats. In March, 1961, President Kennedy's wage bill lost by one vote in the House when too few liberal Republicans rallied to the cause deserted by most conservative Democrats.

In other words, at the national level in American politics there is rarely a strong, internally cohesive majority which is prepared to fight as one man for its policies. Given this fragmentation, this inability to combine for coercive measures, the courts have great leeway for their policy-making activities. Can one imagine, for example, Congress taking any action against the Supreme Court for the decision in the *School Segregation Cases*? On rare occasions, notably during wartime, cohesive, coercive majorities may mobilize, and at this point the courts usually follow a policy of judicious inaction.[11] When, for example, in 1942 the President and the Congress united to lock 75,000 American citizens of Japanese ancestry in concentration camps for possessing enemy chromosomes, the courts stood idly by and eventually the Supreme Court (*Korematsu* v.

United States, 1945) justified the action. A similar example, this one from the Reconstruction period, saw the Court actually deprived of jurisdiction over appeals from *habeas corpus* decisions to prevent it from hindering congressional punishment of the defeated South (*Ex parte McCardle,* 1869).

The point is that there are ways both direct and indirect of bringing pressure against the courts. In the sphere of possible direct action, Congress could do what it did to frustrate appeals from *habeas corpus* decisions in the Reconstruction period: simply forbid appeals from decisions of this type. Indirectly, constant public pressure upon the courts from a mobilized majority in Congress would surely have an impact on even the most independently minded judge, to say nothing of the kind of harassment that the Senate could engage in while fulfilling its task of approving presidential judicial appointments. Senator James Eastland, Chairman of the Senate Judiciary Committee, has for the past few years been waging guerrilla warfare against the Supreme Court from his fortified position because of its decision on school segregation, and his persistent claim that the high Court has been captured by the Communists has undoubtedly caused a great deal of judicial anguish.

Yet, while there have been since the time of Jefferson demands that the wings of the federal judiciary must be clipped, there is no reason to expect that the political functions of the courts, and particularly the Supreme Court, will suddenly be extinguished. An occasional Court decision may be overruled where the justices based their opinion on the alleged intentions of Congress; for example, there has been a drive on for several years to get Congress to announce publicly and statutorily that it did not mean to forbid the states to punish sedition against the nation and thus reverse the Supreme Court's ruling (*Pennsylvania* v. *Nelson,* 1956) that the legislature meant to preëmpt the area when it passed the Smith Act. But until the United States develops a true national party system it can safely be predicted that the courts will retain their ancient prerogative of participating in the determination of public policy. Needless to add, the development of such a disciplined party system seems to be a very remote contingency.

The Federal Judges

Since the federal courts have traditionally had the power to invade the sphere of political decision-making, it is understandable that no President, nor political caucus, has been willing to take the process of judicial appointment "out of politics." To turn the judiciary over to legal experts would be equivalent to letting accountants determine monetary policy. To say this is not to suggest that federal judges generally lack or have lacked legal talent; on the contrary, many of them have been men of impressive ability. It is rather to suggest that political experience, not legal expertise, has usually been the outstanding factor in appointment. In the Senate debate on President Kennedy's 1961 proposal to appoint fifty-nine new federal judges, the Republicans made clear their view that this was a patronage grab. "These judgeships," Senator Dirksen observed, "are really choice patronage products." Senator Russell of Georgia, looking at it from another angle, noted that "the net effect of this will be to increase the malignant influence and tyrannical power of the present Supreme Court." [12]

The political antecedents of the members of the first Supreme Court have already been noted and to emphasize the point let us call the roll of the early Chief Justices. The first was John Jay, who left a distinguished political career in New York for the bench and declined to let his judicial responsibilities hinder his future: while still Chief Justice, he ran in 1795 for Governor of New York, was elected, and resigned from the Court. Washington then appointed John Rutledge of South Carolina, one of the framers of the Constitution, to the post, but the Senate rejected the appointment for political reasons, demonstrating to Thomas Jefferson that "they will receive none but tories hereafter into any Department of the Government." Washington's next two candidates, Patrick Henry and Justice Cushing, declined the honor, but Oliver Ellsworth, the Connecticut Senator who had played a leading part in drafting the Judiciary Act of 1789, accepted and served until 1800.[13]

John Marshall, appointed by President Adams in January 1800, began his career on the Court by simultaneously performing the duties of Chief Justice and Secretary of State for six weeks—indeed, in his capacity as Secretary of State (for which he accepted no salary) he had signed the commission of the unfortunate Marbury which was to to be the *cause célèbre* in 1803. Marshall was a distinguished Virginia politician, a former Congressman, and one-time member of the Virginia Convention which ratified the Constitution. When in 1835 the "great Chief Justice" went to his reward, he was replaced by Roger B. Taney (pronounced Tawney), one of the most controversial political figures of the day.

Taney was nothing more nor less than President Jackson's chief hatchetman. Incidentally, and only incidentally, he was a superb lawyer. His willingness to destroy the Bank of the United States by exercising the right of the Secretary of the Treasury to withdraw federal deposits from its working capital brought upon his head the obloquy of the Senate, which rejected his nomination as Secretary of the Treasury. Jackson, enraged at this rejection of his former Attorney General and interim Secretary of the Treasury, then placed his name in nomination for a Supreme Court justiceship, but again the Senate refused to confirm the appointment. The Clerk of the Senate brought word of this to Jackson, who flew into one of his famous rages and announced that he wanted no message from the "damned scoundrels." After Marshall's death, Jackson tried again, only this time he added insult to injury by nominating Taney for Chief Justice—"Judge (Joseph) Story thinks the Supreme Court is *gone,* and I think so too," observed Senator Daniel Webster. A New York newspaper remarked charitably that Taney was "unworthy of public confidence, a supple, cringing tool of power." [14]

These early political-judicial appointments have been explored a bit because we sometimes suffer under the illusion that politics in the judiciary is a modern invention; that by contrast with our benighted times, in the days of our ancestors great and noble philosopher-statesmen were standard equipment on the federal bench. Having made our point, let us skip a century or so and take a look at the current mode of appointment to the federal courts.

When a vacancy on the District Court level occurs, candidates present themselves much as James Wilson did in 1789. While technically the power to appoint lies with the President, in fact the President seldom gets involved in the proceedings until a candidate has been agreed upon. Occasionally, the President may have to bring about a compromise between rival factions to get a candidate, but generally these problems are worked out by the leaders of the President's party in the state where the vacancy exists. Party loyalty and service are vital considerations, although competence in the law cannot be ignored: a bad nomination can bring down the wrath of the bar associations, the trade-union locals of the legal profession. When, in 1961, the President had the opportunity to appoint over a hundred judges, Attorney General Robert Kennedy announced that the bar associations would be asked to evaluate all nominees in advance of appointment. Once a candidate has been nominated by the President, with the correct party clearance, Senate approval is automatic. In the improbable event that the President should nominate a person over the opposition of a Senator of his party from the appropriate state, "senatorial courtesy" comes into play: the Senator rises, points out that he finds the nominee "unacceptable," and the Senate invariably rejects the nomination.

Once on the federal bench, a judge is expected to break his formal ties with his party. No one, however, anticipates that he will alter the pattern of his private life or change his friends. In fact, as anyone who has been active in politics will testify, federal judges frequently play an important informal role in political organizations. There are a few judges who have followed the British pattern of rigid political neutrality in private as in public life, but, at least at the District Court level, this is atypical.

At the Court of Appeals level (the current structure of United States courts will be explicated in detail in the next section), there is much more emphasis on legal expertise. With the exception of the Court of Appeals in the District of Columbia, all these courts handle appellate work from several states and are thus removed to some extent from local political jurisdictions. A number of appellate judges have been promoted to the intermediate bench from the District courts on the basis of distinguished legal performance, though political factors can never be excluded. Let us put it this way: no President feels impelled to reward his political enemies. Thus if there are two candidates for a position on the Court of Appeals of roughly equal personal and technical qualifications, but of varying party antecedents, a Democratic President will normally appoint the Democrat and the Republican President, the Republican.

Presidents usually have a great deal of leeway in appointing Supreme Court justices, and the basis for nomination may often appear quite eccentric. True, there are certain regional and ethnic rules of an informal character that operate: no American institution is complete without its Catholic and Jewish complement, and the geographic areas of the nation are utilized as rough rules of thumb for purposes of judicial representation. Thus when Justice Pierce Butler, a Midwestern Catholic, died in 1939, President Roosevelt replaced him with Frank Murphy, also Midwestern and Catholic, though holding radically different political and economic views. President Harry Truman had the mystifying habit for one of his generally liberal persuasion of appointing uniformly conservative Supreme Court justices. President Hoover, on the other hand, was accused of packing the Court with radicals; Chief Justice

Taft conveyed to a friend his reluctance to resign, though he was in bad health, until Hoover had been replaced in the White House by a sound Republican. He was convinced the President would replace him with a "Bolshevik." [15] There was considerable uncertainty in informed Washington circles as to the basis for President Eisenhower's appointments; when asked, the President invariably replied that they were "fine Americans."

Judicial Structure Today

As was noted earlier, the judicial structure initiated in the Judiciary Act of 1789 remained in operation, with minor modifications, until 1891. In this year Congress passed the Circuit Courts of Appeals Act which created a new set of courts intermediate between the federal courts of original jurisdiction (District and Circuit courts—the latter were not abolished until 1911) and the Supreme Court. The main task of these Circuit Courts of Appeal was to relieve the Supreme Court of the intolerable burden of appellate business that had been piling up, a burden which had put the Court roughly four years behind in its work. While the titles and the jurisdiction of these appeals courts have been altered in the years since 1891, the reform inaugurated in that year provided us with our contemporary judicial structure, whose basic pattern is indicated in the chart on page 29.[16]

At the base of the judicial system are the United States District Courts, roughly ninety of them, with original jurisdiction. In other words, these courts handle no appeals, but are limited to beginning litigation. Each judicial district has several judges, the number determined by the volume of business and the generosity of Congress; the District Court for the District of Columbia, for example, where a great deal of federal litigation occurs, has today fourteen judges assigned to its work.

District courts handle both criminal and civil actions, that is, both criminal trials for offenses against the laws

THE JUDICIAL SYSTEM

"LEGISLATIVE COURTS" AND ADMINISTRATIVE TRIBUNALS

- initial litigation
-- direct appeal - mandatory
→ appeal at discretion of Supreme Court (certiorari)
--→ (when District holds act of Congress unconstitutional)

(1) N.L.R.B., S.E.C., F.C.C., etc.
(2) Secretary of Agriculture, Administrator of Wage & Hour Law, etc.
(3) Original jurisdiction defined in Article III of Constitution

Boxes in diagram:

COURT OF CUSTOMS AND PATENT APPEALS

COURT OF CUSTOMS.

COURT OF CLAIMS

INDEPENDENT REGULATORY COMMISSIONS (1)

ADMINISTRATIVE ADJUDICATION (2)

UNITED STATES SUPREME COURT (3)

UNITED STATES DISTRICT COURT 3 Judges - (For adjudicating issues of constitutionality)

UNITED STATES COURTS OF APPEAL (Eleven Circuits)

(rare)

UNITED STATES DISTRICT COURTS (Eighty-seven Districts)

FEDERAL COURTS

TOP APPELLATE COURT

INTERMEDIATE APPELLATE COURTS

TRIAL LEVEL

(rare)

STATE COURTS

of the United States and civil actions to which the United States is a party, as for example a lawsuit growing out of a farmer's suing the government for ramming his barn with a B-52 bomber. These are *federal questions:* they are founded on the relationship of the individual to the national government. In addition, District courts handle original suits arising from *diversity jurisdiction,* in which the litigants are citizens of different states. Since corporations have citizenship for these legal purposes, much corporate litigation occurs in the District courts between corporations situated in different states. Congress, which has complete control over the exercise of jurisdiction, has attempted to limit the work of the District courts in diversity cases by providing that only in cases with at least $5,000 at issue can the matter be litigated in the federal forum. Where less than this is at stake, and no matter how authentic the diversity of citizenship may be, the problem must be taken to a state court; state courts have for these purposes been granted jurisdiction.

District courts, besides being vested with civil and criminal authority, also operate in another legal dimension: they are both courts of law and courts of equity. *Equity* was once described as "something you study for two years in law school to learn that nobody knows exactly what it is." Thus to attempt to define it in a few words is unrealistic. Perhaps the best simple definition of equity is *anticipatory retaliation*: one goes to court to prevent some irremediable harm from occurring to him or his interests. For example, the Dean of a university learns that an entrepreneur is planning to build a huge dance hall on a vacant lot across the street from the library—"Bookburners' Lodge"—and rushes to court to stop this menacing threat to the future of education. He applies for an injunction to stop the building until a court can decide whether the university's interests are in fact endangered. On a more serious level, the state of California goes to the Supreme Court to prevent the state of Arizona from taking more water from the

Colorado River and applies for equitable relief. If Arizona were building a new dam, California could wait until the dam was completed, the precious water withheld, and then bring a civil action, but this would be after the fact; it is much better to get the question litigated in advance by applying for judicial relief before damages occur. These are simple and clear-cut cases of equity jurisdiction and will suffice for our discussion. In its complex applications, equity assumes a mystical quality equaled only by Zen Buddhism.

The Constitution established procedural requirements for the federal courts in some detail. In all serious criminal cases, there must first of all be a presentment by a grand jury. That is, before he can even take his case to court for trial, the United States Attorney who represents the Department of Justice in each district must convince a grand jury that there is reasonable ground for the action. If a majority of the grand jury agrees, a "true bill" or indictment is turned in and the matter proceeds to the trial stage. This provision of the Fifth Amendment was designed to forestall any "Star Chamber" judicial prosecutions by agents of the national government—all criminal prosecutions had to be filtered through a local body. Article III, Section 3 of the Constitution requires that all criminal trials be "by Jury," and this has been rigorously construed as demanding unanimous decision of a twelve-person petty jury to convict. Just to make sure that the new leviathan did not escape its moorings, the Fifth and Sixth Amendments added that the accused could not twice be put in jeopardy for the same offense, could not be forced to incriminate himself (a restriction aimed at eliminating any possibility of torture), could not be denied a speedy and public trial, and could not be tried except by an "impartial jury of the State and district wherein the crime shall have been committed." Moreover, he must be informed of the details of the accusation, be confronted by hostile witnesses, have the right to subpoena his own witnesses, and have the right of counsel. This is a formidable arsenal of protective measures and is rigorously enforced in the federal courts.

While they were at it, the authors of the Bill of Rights added a provision (Amendment 7) to inhibit any licentious federal behavior in civil actions. Here they provided that in all "suits at common law" undertaken by federal courts in the exercise of their diversity jurisdiction where the amount at issue was more than $20, the "right of trial by jury shall be preserved." It should be noted that this right to a jury trial, both in criminal and in civil cases, can be waived by the agreement of the parties involved. No juries are employed when courts sit in admiralty or in the exercise of their equity jurisdiction. It is interesting further to note that as a consequence of these constitutional imperatives, the United States is the last stronghold of trial by jury—in Great Britain there are no grand juries, no juries in civil actions, and the right to a jury in criminal trials is limited to a small percentage of serious prosecutions.

The Courts of Appeal

For appellate purposes, the United States is divided into eleven Judicial Circuits, each with a Court of Appeals consisting of a Chief Justice and a varying number of Circuit Judges. The First Judicial Circuit, for instance, takes in the Districts of Maine, New Hampshire, Massachusetts, Rhode Island, and Puerto Rico and has only three judges; the Ninth Judicial Circuit includes Alaska, Washington, Oregon, California, Nevada, Arizona, Idaho, Montana, Hawaii, and Guam and has nine judges to handle its business. A Supreme Court Justice is still assigned to each Circuit (a reminder of the days when the justices, to their dismay, actually rode out into the country to serve on the old Circuit Courts)—but his responsibilities for it are minimal.

The Courts of Appeal have exclusively appellate jurisdiction, *i.e.*, they do no trial work. Their cases come from two sources: first, they hear appeals from the district courts in their bailiwicks, and, second, they handle appeals from the rulings of various administrative tribunals such as the Interstate Commerce Commission and the National Labor Relations Board. Generally speaking, they are not supposed to reëxamine the factual determinations of the agencies or courts below, but are expected to limit their review to matters of law. In practice the distinction between law and fact is often hard to maintain—in many situations the presence or absence of certain facts determines the law to be applied—so that Courts of Appeal may review the whole record and reinterpret the facts for themselves. It is fair to say that they have wide authority to oversee the actions of the District courts and administrative agencies. Congress has by statutes required that appeals from the determinations of certain key administrative agencies must be heard in the Court of Appeals for the District of Columbia, so this body assumes great importance in the judicial structure.

It is hard to generalize about the operation of a Court of Appeals; indeed, almost any broad statement concerning either jurisdiction or structure must be qualified in good legal fashion. Some cases are dealt with by one Circuit Judge, some by three, and on occasion the whole bench of judges may sit *en banc* to determine the outcome of a serious constitutional problem. It is possible for the court as a whole to revise the decision of one of its members. This flexibility, while it troubles lovers of symmetry and precision, makes it possible for these courts to adapt themselves to the needs of different situations. This is very important for the litigant since few cases ever get beyond the appeals level; the Court of Appeals is usually the last stop. On rare occasions, when it is impossible to get a quorum of the Supreme Court (six Justices) to sit in judgment on a case, a Court of Appeals may serve as the final forum. The most famous instance of this, the anti-trust action against ALCOA in 1945, found four Supreme Court Justices disqualifying themselves from sitting in judgment (they had all been associated with the Department of Justice preparations for the lawsuit at one time or another in the past), so the Court exercised its statutory power to refer the matter for final settlement to the Second Circuit Court.[17]

The Supreme Court

The only court mentioned specifically in the Constitution, the Supreme Court began life with a Chief Justice and five Associate Justices. Since then it has once risen to a population of ten (1863), but has from 1870 on been stabilized at nine. While United States District courts have only original jurisdiction, and Courts of Appeal are exclusively appellate, the Supreme Court has both original and appellate authority. In addition, and distinguishing it at this point from the Courts of Appeal, it has the right to review decisions of both federal and state courts. The grounds on which it may overrule state courts will be discussed shortly; suffice it here to note that in this capacity the Court acts as overseer of the division of powers between states and nation.

The original jurisdiction of the Supreme Court was stipulated in the Constitution: "In all Cases affecting Ambassadors, other public Ministers and Consuls, and those in which a State shall be a Party, the Supreme Court shall have original jurisdiction" (Article III, Section 2). In the brief period before the Eleventh Amendment, which forbade the federal courts to entertain suits by private citizens against states, there were three jury trials in the Supreme Court, and in 1950 the state of Louisiana asked the Court to empanel a jury to determine the facts in the tidelands dispute—unsuccessfully. Today the original jurisdiction of the Supreme Court is exercised almost exclusively over suits between the United States and a state, and suits between states.

Supreme Court business on its original docket is very slight; the great proportion of its work is in appellate. It was pointed out earlier that the Court receives appeals from two separate sources; the top state court of competent jurisdiction, and the United States Courts of Appeal. (The United States Court of Claims and the United States Court of Customs and Patent Appeals, two "legislative courts" to be discussed later, are treated as Courts of Appeal for purposes of judicial review.) Let us examine in some detail the circumstances and conditions that must exist before the Supreme Court will intervene.

Prior to 1925, there was a large number of decisions which could be appealed to the Supreme Court as a matter of right, *i.e.,* the Court could not refuse to accept jurisdiction and conduct at least a preliminary examination of the merits. The result was an impossible workload and eventual action by Congress (which, it must be reiterated, has plenary control over the appellate power of the Court) to give the Justices discretionary power over the cases they would adjudicate. Since that date, normal procedure is for an appellant to request a writ of certiorari from the Court. With the request for this writ, he includes a *précis* of the issues involved, attempting to demonstrate that there is a "substantial federal question" at issue in the litigation. Each Supreme Court Justice examines the requests for certiorari from his Circuit (or Circuits—two Justices have two under their wing) and extracts from the huge pile those which he feels have merit. These he circulates among his brethren and if three of them concur in his view, the writ is granted and the case is put on the docket for argument. If he feels the request is "frivolous," or if three other Justices will not agree that a significant question is involved, the writ is rejected. The same procedure is followed with respect to appeals from state courts.[18]

Congress has, however, provided that the Court *must* accept jurisdiction in certain limited categories of cases. First, in the federal jurisdiction, it must entertain an appeal from a decision in a Circuit that a state statute violates the United States Constitution, treaties, or laws. Second, also in the federal forum, it must take direct appeals from any decision in a District Court or Court of Appeals which holds an act of Congress to be unconstitutional (special procedures exist for appealing such a decision directly from the District level to the Supreme Court without stopping at the intermediate station). Third, it must answer appropriate questions of law certified to it by a Court of Appeals when the latter is in doubt about some significant rule of decision (this occurs most frequently when two Circuits have ruled differently on the same issue and the Supreme Court has not spoken authoritatively).

Finally, in the exercise of its supervisory role over the state courts, the Supreme Court *must* hear an appeal, *first,* when a state tribunal has declared an act of Congress or a treaty unconstitutional, and *second,* when a state law has been attacked as violating the United States Constitution and has been sustained by the appropriate state court. A professor of law might quibble about the simplistic wording employed here because each of these provisions is very complicated, but presumably no law professor will be learning federal jurisdiction from this book!

In any event, the Supreme Court today has virtually complete control over its docket: it can pick and choose among the hundreds of requests for certiorari that pour in each year and select only those cases which have significant constitutional or statutory implications.

Judicial Self-Restraint

Over the years, the Supreme Court has adopted certain rules of thumb that it applies to litigation before it. In particular, it has announced a doctrine of humility which is often referred to as judicial self-restraint. Because it does have final authority over so many matters of constitutional and statutory construction—and because it wants to retain this authority—the Court avoids demonstrations of muscle power. If, for example, a litigant at bar has challenged the constitutionality of a state or federal statute, the Court will be very reluctant to rule on the issue if it can interpret the law in such a fashion as to avoid the constitutional impediment. To take a specific instance, when Congress ruled in the Taft-Hartley Act that trade unions could not financially support political parties, the Court so construed the statute as not to apply to the case of a union newspaper which endorsed a Democratic candidate and was widely distributed by the union as campaign literature. Said the Court:

> We are unwilling to say that Congress by its prohibition [Section 304 of the Taft-Hartley Act] against corporations or labor organizations making an "expenditure in connection with any election" of candidates for federal office intended to outlaw such a publication. We do not think [the provision] reaches *such a use* of corporate or labor organization funds. [*United States* v. *C.I.O.,* 335 U. S. 106, 123-4 (1948), emphasis added.]

This sort of decision puts the Court in the mind reading business, and in the case quoted its divination was almost certainly wrong: both Senator Taft and Congressman Hartley announced irately that it was precisely this sort of union activity that they had in mind when they wrote the statute! Since that time, it might be added, the Taft-Hartley provision has been virtually useless.

If the Court looks upon evaluation of constitutionality as a last resort, it also insists on certain other conditions. *First,* the party who appeals must demonstrate that he has "standing," that is, that he has a right to make his claim. If, for instance, he claims that a law has damaged him and it appears that he has not been in fact touched by it, he will be sent on his way unaided. The Supreme Court does not give free advice to citizens on whether they *may* be denied constitutional rights *if* something should happen to them. (As usual, there are rare exceptions when the judges get carried away and do deal with hypothetical issues.) *Second,* and closely related, there must be a "case or controversy," *i.e.,* a genuine legal disagreement in which the conflicting positions are set forth. This does not bar a

test case—many such go before the Court; it does bar
handing the Justices a pig in a poke in which, for example,
the parties litigant have so stipulated the facts as to foreclose
real controversy. To take a semifictitious example, a citizen
goes to the ticket agent at the railroad station, asks to buy
a fare at a new low rate prescribed by the Interstate Commerce Commission. By prearrangement the ticket agent
refuses to sell it to him on the ground that the new rate is
confiscatory and deprives the carrier of property without
due process of law in violation of the Fifth Amendment.
The citizen brings suit in the federal court, agrees that the
new rate *is* confiscatory, but demands his ticket. The record
going up from the District Court, presuming that a court
would entertain the motion, would include a stipulation of
facts to the effect that the new rate was confiscatory and
the Supreme Court would be asked a question equivalent
to the old saw "Do you still beat your wife?" namely, does
a "confiscatory" rate schedule violate the Fifth Amendment? This would *not* be a "case of controversy."

Finally, at least for our purposes here, the Court has
repeatedly since the days of John Marshall avoided "political questions." The extent to which this doctrine is applied
seems to be a direct coefficient of judicial egotism, for the
definition of a "political question" can be expanded or con-
tracted in accordion-like fashion to meet the needs of a
situation. Suffice it to say that if the Court feels that a
question before it, for example, the legitimacy of a state
government, the validity of a legislative apportionment,
or the correctness of executive action in the field of foreign
relations, is one that is not properly amenable to judicial
settlement, it will refer the plaintiff to the "political" organs
of government for possible relief. A precise, juridical definition of "political questions" is impossible, for at root
the logic that supports it is circular: political questions are
matters not soluble by the judicial process; matters not soluble by the judicial process are political questions. As an
early dictionary explained, a violin is a small cello; a
cello is a big violin.[19]

An example may help to point up this ambiguity. According to settled Court doctrine, a citizen can get no redress in the courts of the United States for having his vote depreciated by gerrymandering. There is an amazing variation in population among congressional districts which often can for purposes of federal representation make one man's vote in a small district equal to the vote of three men in a big one. On its face the gerrymander would seem to violate the equal protection clause of the Fourteenth Amendment, but the Supreme Court has held (*Colegrove* v. *Green,* 1946) that the aggrieved citizen must rely on the political process for relief. (The absurdity of this doctrine is apparent: after all, what the citizen is trying to get is an equal shake in the political process and the purpose of the gerrymander is precisely to prevent this. He was in effect told by the Court to use his worthless vote to gain an equal vote!) Yet, while the Court felt incapable of attempting a judicial remedy for the gerrymander, it undertook the arduous task of reforming Southern educational practice by ordering desegregation in the public schools. In short, there are a lot of political questions that are not "political questions" for judicial purposes.

Legislative Courts

By this time the reader may be wondering exactly how many precise statements can be made about the judicial process. All too frequently commentators, in the effort to simplify extremely complex issues, give the impression that judicial or other governmental matters are reducible to precise generalizations. The fact is that anyone who attempts to analyze American government as if it were a hydrocarbon or a problem in algebra is in for a shock. The structure and operation of the American judiciary is mysterious to behold and not the least mystifying component is the so-called "legislative court." The distinction between a "constitutional" and a "legislative" court was invented by Chief Justice John Marshall in one of his more creative moments

(*American Insurance Co.* v. *Canter,* 1828) and has wandered along through American constitutional law ever since, leaving chaos and confusion in its wake. As Marshall defined it, a "legislative court" was a court established by Congress under Article I of the Constitution rather than Article III, and the earmarks of such a court were that it could be given administrative tasks to perform and that its judges did not have life tenure but held office for a term of years.

Now it is settled doctrine that a constitutional court cannot undertake administrative duties—award pensions, issue marriage licenses, enounce industrial regulations (though they do naturalize aliens!)—because such matters are not "cases or controversies," but the converse does not apply: legislative courts can and do undertake judicial functions and in this capacity make decisions which are reviewable by the Supreme Court. The Court of Claims, for example, acts both administratively and judicially; for a while this body was treated as a constitutional court (*Miles* v. *Graham,* 1925), but was later relegated to its pristine status as a legislative court (*Williams* v. *United States,* 1933). Similar confusion dominated the status of the courts of the District of Columbia: for years they were treated as legislative courts with constitutional functions; then in 1933 the order was reversed and they were held to be constitutional courts with legislative extracurricular duties. John Marshall's inventiveness really opened Pandora's box.

The duties undertaken by the courts do not therefore determine in any exact fashion their status. Neither does the tenure of their judges. Although one can state flatly that any federal judge who holds office for a stated term is on a legislative court (Tax Court, twelve years; territorial judges in the Virgin Islands, four years; etc.) the judges of the Court of Claims, the Court of Customs and Patent Appeals, the Customs Court have life tenure assuming "good behavior." The simplest thing to do is accept the fact that there are legislative courts, that the distinction between a legislative and a constitutional court is often difficult even for the Supreme Court to rationalize, and let it go at that. They are useful.

Independent Regulatory Commissions and Federal Administrators

As any careful analysis of the federal administrative structure demonstrates, large chunks of judicial power are deposited in the hands of various agents and agencies varying from the Secretary of Agriculture and the Administrator of the Wage and Hour Law to the Interstate Commerce Commission and the Federal Aviation Agency. Of course, the Department of Defense has control, subject to review by a special tribunal, the United States Court of Military Appeals, of the justice dispensed in the armed services. Back in the old days, when constitutional purists could not bear to look the facts of administrative law in the face, it was established that these bodies had "quasijudicial powers." This is an interesting example of judicial semantics: the settled opinion was that it would violate the separation of powers if executive agencies exercised judicial power— therefore the powers these organs did in fact utilize could not be judicial, but had to be "softened by a quasi" (Holmes, J., dissenting in *Springer* v. *Government of Philippine Islands,* 1928).

As matters now stand, it is likely that for each American who goes to court for a settlement of his difficulties, a hundred or more receive redress at the hands of administrative tribunals. For example, the Internal Revenue Service annually turns up thousands of questionable income tax returns, the overwhelming percentage of which are settled administratively by "quasijudicial" decisions of authorized bureaucrats. Only when a citizen thinks he has a strong case, and plenty of income for lawyers (a deductible business expense!), will the case actually emerge in a federal court as a civil suit. (Only when it is demonstrable that the tax deficiency was due to willful action with intent to defraud the government does the criminal process enter the picture.)

That these determinations are only "quasijudicial" in no way softens their impact or consequences: they are enforceable and binding unless overruled by a body with competent jurisdiction. What administrative adjudication provides is rapid and, usually, inexpensive settlement of the innumerable conflicts that arise in a society as tightly organized and highly structured as ours today. To follow the old procedure of litigating every tax argument in the federal courts would block all other business with an annual load of tax cases that could in itself take years of judicial work. What is needed is fast yet equitable decision-making and, although the leaders of the bar have disputed the point for years, there is no reason why an administrator cannot be as judicious as a judge. Moreover, as one chosen for his expert knowledge of a substantive field—labor relations, taxation, immigration rules, agriculture—the administrative "judge" does not have to begin each case at zero. To take a specific instance, a federal judge hearing a radio patent case is supposed to acquire sufficient expertise in electronics to decide who stole what ideas from whom. His next patent case, eight months later, leaves him high and dry with his painfully acquired information about electronics: he is to determine whether or not there has been an infringement of a patented process for solar heating systems. The Examiner from the National Labor Relations Board who holds a hearing in a factory on unfair labor practices has, by contrast, spent his working life in the area and can, if talented, not only spot the objective criteria which are essential, but can also sense the environmental conditions which so often make the difference between justice and injustice in a specific case.

It is, however, essential that these administrative adjudicators be given special status in their organizations. Basic to the principles of "natural justice"—to use the British term—or administrative due process is the old proposition formulated by John Locke that "no man shall be a judge in his own cause." In other words, the men charged with judicial duties must be given special protection, notably from the wrath of their agency superiors, so they can proceed to the handling of individual cases without being "house men." Congress has in the past twenty years wrestled with this problem and has moved a considerable distance in the direction of setting up judicial enclaves within administrative agencies, providing that those men who undertake judicial functions shall have wide autonomy. Ideally Congress should adopt the position advanced in the 1930's by many distinguished American administrative lawyers and establish in each department an administrative court, which would not be part of the hierarchy but would be solely charged with handling disputes arising from the agency's administrative responsibilities. Congress has so far refused to do this, though it has moved in this direction, because the leaders of the lawyers' lobby, the American Bar Association, have sternly denied the validity of any adjudication which does not occur in a courtroom. Despite the fact that it was not anticipated by the founders of the Republic, administrative law and administrative adjudication are here to stay, and the wise course would be to establish the best possible system, not to run around firing off popguns at "administrative tyranny." [20]

The Law of the Federal Courts

We have examined in some detail the agencies charged with the application of judicial power. It now becomes necessary, in conclusion, to discuss briefly the law that these bodies utilize in their day-to-day activities. Alas, this too is very complicated and we can only attempt here to set out the major propositions that apply.

Federal law is set forth in two huge compilations, the Criminal Code and the Civil Code. As legal codes go, these are reasonably straightforward, but—because no legislation can possibly anticipate all future events—massive problems of interpretation often arise. To take a neat and fascinating question: can a corporation which is wholly owned by one man invoke the self-incrimination provisions of the Fifth Amendment? If the individual concerned were *as a person* asked certain questions, he clearly could refuse to answer under the terms of the Fifth Amendment. But suppose that, as the sole owner of the corporation, he is asked the same questions *in his corporate capacity*. Can he correctly refuse to testify? Or must he answer even if his answers incriminate him in his personal capacity? The reader who finds this intriguing can find the answer in the Supreme Court *Reporter!* [21]

Taking another problem (from the seamier side of life), can a bookmaker, who operates in violation of state law but pays federal income taxes on his profits, deduct the cost of his (illegal) horse-room as a business expense? [22] Or, what is the application of the federal loyalty program? Did Congress mean to ensure that a Communist washroom attendant at the Lincoln Memorial be dismissed on the same basis as an atomic physicist at Hanford? Or, what is "coercion" in a labor dispute? All these, and thousands like them, arrive in the federal courts for adjudication—largely as a consequence of the skeletal character of most acts of Congress. Congress typically, and wisely, passes a statute drawn in general terms and leaves the specific implementation to some agency of the government. However, this always leaves open the subsequent question: has the agency in fact followed the will of Congress, or has it deviated from the true principles of the legislation and gone into business for itself? Much judicial time and energy thus goes into congressional mindreading.

Yet dealing with the intent of Congress is a kindergarten problem by comparison with the difficulties that arise in diversity jurisdiction. To recapitulate, a federal court is seized (to use legal language) of jurisdiction over a suit between citizens of different states, providing certain other conditions are present. Let us hypothesize a suit between a citizen of New York and a citizen of California, brought in the federal district court in Los Angeles, for $100,000 on breach of contract. Here the federal judge would apply the California law of contract; in the event that there is some tricky aspect of the California law of contract which might be decisive in the issue, he must accept as binding the interpretation of this statute by the highest state court that has ruled upon the matter. Suppose this decision is murky at key points? Or that two courts of equal weight have ruled differently and there has been no resolution by the California Supreme Court? Then life gets complicated, and it is a regular event for a Court of Appeals to correct a federal district judge's interpretation of a state law or a state judicial decision. (By the way, one of the arguments for drawing district judges from local legal circles is their acquaintance with state law.)

Moreover, in diversity cases, while they utilize state law, federal courts employ federal procedures, uniformly determined throughout the nation. On its face, this may not seem troublesome until it is remembered that on occasion procedure and substance get a bit confused. For example, a federal rule of evidence (procedural) may destroy the substantive impact of a state law governing contracts by establishing completely different standards of admissibility. It is at times like these that one wishes that the Supreme Court had a larger percentage of brilliant legists; indeed, of the present bench, only Justice (sometime professor) Felix Frankfurter knows his way surely through such labyrinths, and his colleagues are often reluctant to follow his slightly pedagogical trail.

The student who decides to attend law school will find himself face to face with these intricate by-products of federalism soon enough; suffice it here to note that the federal courts must not only apply and interpret appropriate federal sanctions to the cases at bar, but also in diversity jurisdiction be experts on the laws of the several states. From time to time, the Supreme Court itself must take time out to wrestle with such a monumental question as: Did the United States District Court, Southern District of New York, correctly interpret the ruling of the New York State Court of Appeals on the state law of trespass? In fairness it should be added that this is rare—the Court seldom grants certiorari in a case of this character unless there is conflict below, *i.e.,* the Court of Appeals has overruled the district on the legal point.

Conclusions

To summarize, there are several aspects of the American judicial process that must be highlighted:

First, in many crucial political matters, the federal judges are part of the decision-making process. Utilizing the traditional right of judicial review under the Constitution, it is possible for a state justice of the peace, if vested with jurisdiction by state law, to declare an act of Congress or an action of the President of the United States unconstitutional. Judges cannot therefore be considered as legal technicians since potentially they are capable of decisive intervention in the policy-making activities of the so-called political sector—the executive and the legislature.

Second, it is submitted that the major reason that judges have been able to exercise this enormous jurisdiction over public policy is the absence of a disciplined, internally cohesive national two-party system. No strongly organized political majority would permit for long the dabbling in policy by irresponsible, nonelected, permanent officials. It is precisely the fluidity of our party system that has provided the judiciary with its political elbowroom.

Third, the federal judiciary and the Supreme Court in particular must be examined as a component of the political sector, though in all likelihood the overwhelming bulk of judicial decisions have no political consequences. Operating in this capacity—as a political body—the Supreme Court has served as a permanently sitting constitutional convention which has revised the antique document at crucial points in terms of the exigent needs of new eras. It is probably because they sensed its importance as the mechanism of social adjustment that Presidents have traditionally reserved its seats for veterans of the political arena, for men who realize that, in the words of former Chief Justice Hughes, "the Constitution is what the judges say it is."

Finally, judicial power is not limited to federal judges, but is distributed widely throughout the operational structure of our government. While the federal courts always (or, to put in the last of many lawyer's quibbles, almost always) have the power to review these "quasijudicial" decisions, for the average citizen the judicial power of the Treasury Department or the Department of Agriculture is far more immediate than that of the District court or Supreme Court.

- 3 -

THE RIGHTS OF THE CITIZEN

A useful way of testing a society's actual dedication to the principles of freedom and democracy is to ascertain in precise institutional terms the personal rights of the citizen. Many nations have abstractly gone on record as devout supporters of the inalienable rights of man, but have overlooked incorporating these rights into the practical, enforceable laws of the land. In France, where sonorous accolades to liberty have been the fashion for a century and a half, nobody before de Gaulle ever got around to establishing the writ of habeas corpus, that neat legal instrument which forces a jailer to prove that his detention of a prisoner is legally justified. In India, the internal security statute provides that a prisoner can be held for a year before he is booked (that is, before any specific charge is laid against him), thus making possible a one-year deep freeze of political undesirables before instituting formal legal action against them. (Often they are simply released without ever being formally booked.)

In other words, if one is going to examine the content of civil rights, he must penetrate the rhetoric to the practice, must discover not only the slogans and social myths but also the conduct of anonymous police in slum precincts. Part of the reality can be assessed by examining judicial decisions on the subject, but this evidence must be treated with caution. All marriages which do not end in divorce are not necessarily happy; for every instance in which a court insists on a citizen's receiving his rights there may be a hundred cases which are not litigated. It is not unjust to suggest that the greatest single area of violation of civil rights is police practices, but because of the character, poverty, and ignorance of the victims, few cases in this sphere are litigated. Until in recent years the spotlight was focused on the problem, standard police procedure in dealing with Negro, Italian, and Puerto Rican "gangs" of juvenile delinquents was to take them to the station house, beat the ears off them, and then send them home to muse on the evils of sin. While the police involved would admit that an innocent lad occasionally got pushed around, they basically endorsed the philosophy of the French *gendarme* that everyone in the world has at least one beating coming to him.

We will return to this problem later in more detail; what is important here is to note the danger in an excessively legalistic approach to civil liberties which treats the issue as though the only deprivations that occur are those which get litigated in court. Long ago, Socrates was invited by a friend to worship at the temple of the sea-god and see the wonderful gifts which had been provided by those sailors saved from drowning by the god's intervention. Socrates, who knew a bad sample when he saw one, inquired, "Where are the gifts from those who drowned?"

The Heritage of the Common Law

There has been a great deal of loose talk, particularly at legal banquets, about the libertarian heritage of the common law. Unfortunately, the history of the common law fails to support most of these generalizations. It is true that *historically* there did emerge from the British legal tradition, particularly by contrast with the civil law tradition of Continental jurisprudence, a set of legal institutions which contributed to the development of personal liberty. But this was hardly by design—indeed, it was the considered view of the greatest historian of the common law, Frederic

W. Maitland, that the liberty of the subject (citizen, in American parlance) was a fortunate historical accident.[1]

A few examples may help make the point. The jury system, often acclaimed as the fundamental buttress of personal liberty, began its life on an entirely different level. Initially it was a body of the king's subjects charged with informing on their neighbors.

> Let a meet be held in every Wapentake, let the 12 senior thegns go out, and the reeve with them, and let them swear on a relic that they will accuse no innocent man nor conceal any guilty one.
> —Law of Wantage, enacted by Ethelred the Unready (968?-1016)[2]

When a royal justice in eyre (on circuit around Britain) arrived in a locality, the jury was called together to help the king maintain his peace, *i.e.*, his royal right to an untroubled realm. Gradually, over the centuries, the jury was transformed into a check on royal caprice and despotism. It was often a risky business: the judge could throw the whole jury into jail for finding the wrong verdict![3] In other words, the jury was altered from an instrument of royal authority to an instrument of community sentiment. From a libertarian viewpoint, this is not necessarily much of an improvement: communities are not necessarily more tolerant of nonconformity than are judges. Indeed, in seventeenth-century Britain juries were notoriously more ferocious toward Catholics than were Stuart judges.

Similarly, there was no room in the common law for freedom of speech or of the press. True, one could always speak his mind and take his chances, but this is hardly freedom in any meaningful sense. As late as the seventeenth century, Members of Parliament were thrown into the Tower for expressing discordant views *in* the House of Commons, and the subject who expounded political theory at the parish pump might well end up with his ears cropped and his tongue bored with a hot iron. As far as freedom of publication was concerned, the great triumph of the common law was the elimination of prior censorship, *i.e.*, licensing provisions. Once a book or tract was printed, its author was on his own and could be brutally punished for seditious libel, an action in which the jury's *only* function was to determine whether he did in fact publish the document. (Since the purpose of seditious libel laws was to protect the King's Peace, the fact that an alleged libel was true only until 1792 exacerbated the offense: the more truthful it was, the more seditious, *i.e.*, the more likely to cause tumult.)[4]

It must be emphasized that the common law was not constant over time; it was a vast body of charters, statutes of the realm, proclamations, judicial decisions, local customs, and miscellaneous sweepings from here and there, amorphous and sprawling. Under the common law in effect at the time the American Constitution was written, the right to defense by counsel existed only in misdemeanors and treason cases. Originally in both treasons and felonies ("the only adequate definition of felony seems to be . . . an offense which occasions a total forfeiture of either lands, goods, or both, at the common law; and to which capital or other punishment may be superadded according to the degree of guilt" IV *Blackstone* ★ 95; a misdemeanor, conversely, is any offense less than felonious) the accused was flatly and absolutely denied legal assistance. The logic behind denying counsel in these serious offenses was perverse indeed: it was thought to be an insult to the king's judges to suggest that the accused needed help in obtaining justice! [5]

In 1695, as a consequence of unrest among the gentry at the hanging spree which had enlivened the latter part of the century and which had seen each faction employing the law of treason to destroy its enemies whenever an opportunity presented itself, Parliament authorized counsel in treason trials. Not until 1836, however, was this right extended to accused felons, and it must be recalled that under the condign standards of the time there were an appalling number of felonies: a pickpocket often ended on the gallows, or, as public opinion grew more gentle, on a transport bound for the wastes of Australia or the American plantations.

This is not the place to recount the sadistic horrors of the common law, a system which employed the fearful process of outlawry (which declared a man legally beyond the law and authorized his destruction without legal penalty) as a common means of collecting debts and which employed a technique of capital punishment literally too horrible to describe. What is important for our purposes is to discover the contribution that this legal structure made to the tradition of liberty. In this regard, three points can be made.

First, the common law was based on the accusatory rather than the inquisitory mode of procedure. Someone brought a charge against someone else and the royal judge and the jury had the function of finding the truth between them. Admittedly the judges in treason and sedition cases —cases in which the royal prerogative was at issue—were less than impartial arbiters. However in theory it was their function in all cases to dispense justice under God and the law. The inquisitorial technique, which found its way from Justinian's Code into Continental law, put the judge in a different role: as royal prosecutor, he interrogated witnesses under oath, put them to the torture (the common law did not admit torture),[6] and acted without the mitigation of a jury. Out of this often fragile distinction there developed a tradition that the British judge was not merely a royal hatchetman and that British justice was not just a system of royal oppression. To state the matter a little differently, the common law, and a series of great justiciars and judges, set in motion the noble ideal of a government under law in which the crown had the obligation to guarantee justice to litigants and was, indeed, itself treated as no more than a private litigant in some actions. Though in practice the ideal was often sullied, the royal judge became accepted in public mythology as an umpire, not as an agent of kingly despotism.

Second, the common law was a lawyers' paradise, a maze of intricate procedures, pleadings, writs. Someone once described Fascist Italy as 20 per cent totalitarian and 80 per cent inefficient; much the same analysis could be applied to the rigors of the common law. Not that the outcome was not bloody enough—it was. But it could have been so much worse without the ingenuity of the lawyers which supplied the cushion. One can write off the legal profession, as the Puritans did, as entrepreneurs in original sin, but the fact remains that under the sturdy encouragement of the common law there developed in Britain and wherever the common law later wandered, a vigorous legal élite dedicated to procedural regularity—hence opposed to capricious, arbitrary exercises of authority. Few lawyers were ever disturbed by a good hanging, but the whole profession would fly into a rage if improper procedures had preceded it. The common law, in short, was lawyers' law, not administrators' law (as was the French civil law, for example), and this emphasis on proper procedures is surely one of the major foundation-stones of the libertarian edifice. Maitland was fond of observing that the history of freedom must be sought in writs, not rights, *i.e.,* legal procedures were more significant than rhetoric, and the lawyers were in the writ business (a writ was the formal method of bringing action at common law).

Third, the common law supplied a mass of specific institutional forms which could be adapted to the needs and defense of a free society. It was superlatively elastic. The jury's progression into an instrument of community judgment has already been alluded to; the writs of habeas corpus, *quo warranto,* mandamus, certiorari, all employed to prevent arbitrary administrative action, were equally conformable to the requirements of republican justice. The presumption of innocence, a frequently neglected but theoretically authentic component of common-law jurisprudence, fitted neatly into the preconceptions of a society espousing natural rights. In sum, our ancestors had the legal tools at hand and the lawyers to use them—all that

was necessary was to revitalize the British tradition with
the spirit of republican liberty and set to work. As Chief
Justice Tilghman of Pennsylvania put it in 1813:

"Every country has its Common Law. Ours is composed
partly of the Common Law of England and partly of our
own usages. When our ancestors emigrated from England,
they took with them such of the English principles as were
convenient for the situation in which they were about to
place themselves. It required time and experience to ascertain how much of the English law would be suitable
to this country. By degrees, as circumstances demanded, we
adopted English usages, or substituted others better suited
to our wants, till at length before the time of the Revolution we had formed a system of our own." [7]

The Colonial Conception of Civil Liberties

Leaving the general discussion of the British heritage,
let us now turn to the American scene. It is important immediately to confess that there was no miraculous transformation in the common law occasioned by the transatlantic
voyage. Although there were substantial alterations in procedures, largely based on legal ignorance (lawyers were
hardly interested in emigrating until there was an adequate
supply of paying clients, and besides there was a strong
Puritan bias against their devious ways), the most important
change was long-range and accidental.[8] Of necessity, the
administration of royal justice in the colonies had to be
turned over to the colonists themselves: there was no
organized civil service to supply trained judges or administrators and it was not until 1697 that Courts of Vice-
Admiralty were established with personnel directly appointed from England. (These were not common law
courts, but had extensive jurisdiction over maritime and
customs actions; it is interesting to note that they were
deeply resented in the colonies and the public reason advanced in attacking them was the absence of a jury in their
deliberations.)

The consequence of American isolation, a concomitant both of the difficulty in communications and of the British preoccupation with Continental wars, was the growth of a tough, home-grown judicial system built around the jury of right-thinking colonials, and the local justice of the peace. True, the royal governor and his council usually constituted the top appellate court in the colony, but in any judicial system, the real day-to-day power is at the bottom. In effect, the countryside was in control of the colonial élite: they supplied the justices of the peace, the jurors, and the members of the colonial assembly. And as the seventeenth century moved into the eighteenth, and the lawyers began to flourish, there was hardly a time when some dispute was not raging between the colonists and the royal governors over the rights of the settlers. Did the British Habeas Corpus Act extend to the Americans? Could the colonial assemblies establish by their own authority rules of procedure?

And so it went, with the royal authority usually being undermined in fact, if not in theory—and the colonists were willing to settle for facts and leave the theoretical problem to others with leisure to worry about abstractions. The king, back across the Atlantic, had, in addition to extreme measures such as sending in troops, two indirect legal weapons at his disposal: he could disallow acts of colonial legislatures, and he (or, more precisely, the Judicial Committee of his Privy Council) could reverse colonial judicial decisions. But he and his officials were remote from the day-to-day political realities of the colonies and the colonists actually had in their hands the critical power of local initiative. A characteristic trick, employed by our legislatures when they had reason to suspect a law of their choice was dubiously valid in terms of British practice, was the enactment of two-year statutes. Since the process of appeal to Britain took about two years, these measures would expire just about the time the royal councillors were reaching a decision on their standing. The legislature would then reënact the same sub-

stantial provisions in different terms, thus technically requiring a separate process of appeal for another two years
—and the merry game continued. Colonial judges operated
on the same principle of calculated indifference, knowing
that the royal governor (who depended on the local assembly for his "supply," *i.e.,* his pay) was a chained lion
and the Judicial Committee of His Majesty's Privy Council
half a world away.

There thus developed in the American settlements a set
of propositions which men took for granted and considered
their rightful liberties.[9] But it is important to note that
these doctrines were not abstract affirmations of the rights
of man in general, but legalistic arguments supporting the
rights of Englishmen, settled in America, against despotic
usurpation. It is hard, for example, to find a colonial
spokesman who backed the religious autonomy of Roman
Catholics, but there was overwhelming general support
for the specific proposition that no Anglican bishops should
be sent over to unify an American religious establishment.
It is deceptive to term this "nationalism"; the colonial
spokesmen indeed felt they were speaking for *all* Englishmen, not just for those on the Atlantic frontier. More
properly colonial doctrine was founded on the resentment
of very homogeneous and successful groups who detested
outside interference in their affairs, which they felt (correctly) they were handling admirably.

What occurred with regard to the British legal system
was not so much a sharp shift in content as it was a shift
in the locus of judicial power. The steel frame of
centralized administration which the Tudor monarchs had
so laboriously constructed, in which judicial power was one
of the main components, was never instituted on these
shores. Instead, the king effectively lost control of his
judicial system to the localities, to the local élite who may
not have known much law, but knew what they wanted
accomplished. As Lord Townshend informed the Lords of
Trade in 1728: "these people are not so well qualified (from
lack of education) even to serve upon juries, and much

less to act upon a Bench of Judicature. It seems impractica-
ble to provide a remedy until a sufficient revenue is found
amongst them to support the charge of sending judges
from England to take the Circuits by turn in the several
Colonies. . . ." [10] One can imagine the enthusiasm with
which the colonists would have rallied to raise money for
this purpose!

Civil liberty therefore meant noninterference in the
American status quo. It had little to do with individual
rights to freedom of speech, religion, assembly, or publication—unless the British happened to be the oppressors.
What Americans did to minorities in their midst was their
business and had absolutely no relationship to civil liberty.
Patrick Henry, for instance, could demand on behalf of
the Virginians "Give me liberty, or give me death!" but
he was quite prepared to outlaw any Virginian who verbally
supported the rights of the crown, *i.e.*, exercised the liberty
of dissenting from Henry. When the Revolution came,
this attitude was implemented in savage state laws directed
at Tory sedition and conspiracy which went far beyond
the legitimate goal of inhibiting royalist insurrections to
suppress speech and punish opinions. Note, for example,
the broad sweep of the New York treason law of 1781:

> "That if any Person being a Citizen or Subject of this
> State, or of any of the United States of America, . . . shall
> maliciously, advisedly and directly, by preaching, teaching,
> speaking, writing, or printing, declare or maintain, that the
> King of Great Britain hath, or of right ought to have, any
> Authority, or Dominion, in or over this State, or the
> Inhabitants thereof, . . . and shall be convicted thereof,
> shall be adjudged guilty of Felony . . . ." [11]

Virginia similarly, though less severely, punished "any
word, open deed, or act" in support of the royal jurisdiction. Tories and neutrals were well advised to keep their
mouths shut; one basic right the Americans obviously
wanted was that of making their own unjust laws!

The Bill of Rights

Against this background, the Bill of Rights takes on a somewhat different aspect than is usually emphasized. Rather than being designed as the armor of the free citizen, these first ten amendments to the Constitution were the result of the strong desire of many state governments to eliminate in advance the growth of a national judicial administration patterned on the British model. Recall the fact that the colonial élite (while considerably weaker on the history of political theory than is sometimes suggested) were intimately acquainted with the function and potential power of administration and were extremely well versed in what might be called the Whig view of British history, the view which looked on the growth of the centralized administration under royal auspices as the archenemy of the liberties of the subject.

The new institutions established by Articles I and II of the Constitution, the Congress and the Presidency, seemed safely to check each other, and the Senate (plus the double lock on equal state representation in the Senate, *viz.*, the last sentence of Article V) was there to see that state interests were not invaded. But what about the new national judicial machinery authorized by Article III? Could this not become the backbone of a national system of administrative–judicial despotism, operating directly upon the citizen and even on the sovereign states themselves? What would prevent federal judges from setting up a new Star Chamber (Star Chamber was a quasijudicial body created by the Tudors and employed by them and the Stuarts until it was abolished by Parliament in 1641; it operated forcefully, summarily, and directly as an instrument of royal power with none of the procedural restraints of the common law) suppressing hostile newspapers, punishing political opponents, and otherwise despotically advancing the interests of the central government?

The Bill of Rights, then, reflected this concern for the

federal principle and not any abstract American dedication
to freedom of the press, a fair trial, or humane and usual
punishment. In fact, since the First Amendment was directed only at Congress, there was nothing to prevent any
state from establishing, say, Congregationalism as the state
church and hanging Catholics, Unitarians, or atheists (except possibly a state bill of rights). In the same manner,
although Congress was forbidden to interfere with freedom of the press, there were many state laws which did
precisely this. As Leonard W. Levy has demonstrated,
common law restrictions of freedom of speech and press
were taken for granted by the Founding Fathers.[12] The
procedural requirements which Amendments IV, V, VI,
VII, and VIII imposed on the national judiciary were far
more rigid than those in practice in the states. True, these
amendments reflected a concern for civil liberty, but a
civil liberty interpreted institutionally, not personally. The
body politic was to be guarded from despotism; the body of
the individual was left to the discretion of his neighbors and
his state government. That this is not an overstatement
can be adduced from the interesting fact that when in
1798-99 the Federalist administration used the Sedition
Act, passed by Congress in 1798, to suppress the Jeffersonian newspapers, the Jeffersonian leaders denounced
the statute as unconstitutional, as a violation of states'
rights. They had nothing against state sedition acts, or
state prosecutions at common law for seditious libel which
were more severe than the federal law in that they did
not permit truth as a defense against libel; but a national
sedition act was an illegal encroachment on the jurisdiction
of the states.[13]

Abolitionist Jurisprudence

It is fascinating to trace the growth and elaboration of
a legal proposition, and no proposition is more interesting
to examine than the view that the United States Constitution guarantees to every person within our jurisdiction

certain fundamental civil liberties. These are not civil
liberties in the sense we have been discussing that term
heretofore; the concern now is not with the defense of
society from centralized despotism, but the defense of the
individual from his own society. This latter relationship
did not trouble the founders of the Republic who seem
subconsciously to have accepted John Locke's view that if
the nonconformist didn't like it in society, he could and
should go elsewhere. (In Carl Sandberg's version, the
Irish cop in Denver says to the Pawnee Indian anarchist,
"If you don't like it here, go back where you come
from.")[14] Moreover, this was not idle rhetoric: America
was an open society geographically speaking so that if a
Presbyterian found life among Anglicans a little trying, he
could move on to a Presbyterian settlement—and perhaps
rough up the Anglicans a bit.[15]

The first group really to develop a massive ideology of
individual constitutional liberty was the abolitionist movement. Although it is often treated as a group of narrow-
minded, bigoted zealots, the abolitionist movement actually
contained many of the finest minds of early nineteenth-
century America, and several first-rate legal artisans. It is
difficult to communicate to a generation which takes mass
slaughter as a standard component of the human condition
and looks on individual heroism as an antiquated, somewhat tedious quality the kind of dedication to an ideal
which led abolitionist agents in the 1830's, 1840's, and
1850's to go South and work for the liberation of the
slaves. And what a reception they got from local committees of slaveholders! The whip, the tarpot, and the
noose were standard equipment for Southern citizens defending their "peculiar institution." [16] In Northern cities,
the working class, a group with strong preferences for
direct action, also took a dim view of emancipation of
the slaves: they did not want competition from cheap
Negro labor. (In the same spirit, the American Federation
of Labor was from 1890 to 1925 a militant supporter of
restrictive immigration policies.) William Lloyd Garrison,

the unlovable but inflexibly courageous abolitionist, was mobbed in several Northern cities, and others shared his experiences.

With the legalistic emphasis that is characteristically American, the abolitionists instituted a wide-ranging (and sometimes contradictory) attack on the society which permitted this sort of mob rule.[17] Naturally enough, they employed every argument that came to hand (including states' rights—against the Fugitive Slave Law!), but for our purposes the important thing was their utilization of the due process clause of the Fifth Amendment. This they pulled out of the oblivion in which it was resting and converted into a national guarantee of the liberties of the individual citizen and of the Negro. To achieve this goal, they cheerily turned the intention of the Fifth Amendment on its head. As we have noted, the clear purpose of the Bill of Rights was to *limit* the jurisdiction of the *general* government; abolitionist spokesmen interpreted it as limiting the power of the states and effectively enlarging the jurisdiction of the national government. The fact that Chief Justice Marshall had held (*Barron* v. *Baltimore,* 1833) that the provisions of the Fifth Amendment acted only as checks on national power did not disturb them a bit; they completely ignored the holding. The following quotation from an abolitionist tract by George Mellen (*An Argument on the Unconstitutionality of Slavery, Embracing an Abstract of Proceedings in the National and State Conventions on This Subject,* 1841) gives the essence of the argument. In order to protect personal liberty, Mellen argued,

"it was found necessary [in the Constitution] for the states to surrender, in the last resort, the liberty of the individual to the care of the general government, that, when the states could not or would not protect him, then the general government, with its ample abilities and powers, could step in and do it; . . . the result was and is that each and every individual in the country could, and can, look to the general government of the United States for the preservation of his inalienable rights, . . ."[18]

In the hands of such able publicists as Theodore Weld and James G. Birney, the concept of constitutionally guaranteed individual liberties became a major abolitionist slogan and was spread far and wide in the tracts of these indefatigable workers for the Lord. Although, constitutionally speaking, the argument was clearly specious, it nonetheless had a tremendous impact on the antislavery generation, most particularly on the Civil War radicals who eventually drafted the first civil rights acts and the Fourteenth Amendment. While the life and hard times of the Fourteenth Amendment will be examined shortly, it is worth noting that that Amendment was the work of men steeped in abolitionist jurisprudence who were remodeling the Constitution to ensure that individual liberty, for both whites and Negroes, would henceforth be safe from the rapacious incursions of both hostile state governments and hostile citizenry. It should also be noted on a more practical level that the radical Republicans hoped to use the newly enfranchised Negroes to build their party's strength in the Southern states—altruism had in the context of 1865-76 a significant political purpose.

The Modern Development of Civil Rights

The history of civil rights in the United States is a fascinating subject, but obviously one beyond the scope of this volume. However, before we examine the basic rules which operate today, it is essential to examine briefly the instrument of expansion of civil rights and the process by which this growth took place. Involved here is the rise of so-called substantive due process, and the key to expansion lay in the due process clause of the Fourteenth Amendment. In the pre-Civil War period, oddly enough, both the abolitionists and the extreme proslavery zealots advocated substantive due process, that is, they urged that the due process clause of the Fifth Amendment was a limitation on the substance of government power rather than on its form.

This distinction is perhaps best demonstrated by a specific

case—congressional power over the territories. The classic view of due process was that Congress had the authority to establish rules and regulations subject only to the specific limitations of the Constitution as to procedures, *e.g.*, it could not eliminate trial by jury or enact *ex post facto* laws (*Murray* v. *Hoboken Land Co.*, 1856). In other words, nobody could be deprived of his life, liberty, or property *except by established consitutional procedures*. In dealing with the slavery problem, Congress initially provided that in all territories north of the line 36°30' slaveholding was forbidden; in those territories south of the line, it was permitted. In the 1840's the abolitionists moved into high gear, asserting the absurdity of a geographical definition of morality. They claimed that the Missouri Compromise was unconstitutional as a violation of the Fifth Amendment: slavery deprived men and women of liberty without *any* process of law, was inherently immoral and incompatible with the law of the land. Proslavery spokesmen drew the same sword: the Missouri Compromise was unconstitutional in that it deprived men who went north of 36°30' of their property without adjudication. The latter view was adopted by Chief Justice Taney in that monument to judicial egotism, the *Dred Scott Case* (1857).

The Dred Scott decision was a freak, and does not deserve serious treatment on its merits any more than does *Marbury* v. *Madison*. For one thing, the Court split nine ways: two Justices dissented, one in effect said "count me out," and the other six agreed only that Scott, a freed Negro, was not a citizen of Missouri entitled to sue a citizen of New York in the federal courts. For another, it has never been agreed among scholars whether Taney's remarks on the unconstitutionality of the Missouri Compromise were a necessary part of his opinion or an *obiter dictum* (the legal term for a judicial excursion into matters not essential to the holding). But the concept of substantive due process, as Howard Jay Graham has shown in a series of superb essays, was rattling around both in legal circles and in some state courts.[19]

Graham has also demonstrated to my satisfaction that the framers of the Fourteenth Amendment were men who considered substantive due process to be an essential component of constitutionalism. Without getting involved in the talmudic controversy over whether the Amendment was designed to apply the exact provisions of the Bill of Rights to the states, it is safe to say that its central purpose was to protect certain natural rights from state infringement. The radical Republicans who drew it up were strong supporters of the view that all humans were born with certain inviolable substantive rights (speech, opinion, press, assembly, religion, and property) which it was the obligation of the national government to protect from *all* enemies, public or private. While in the context of Reconstruction the emphasis was naturally on the protection of the newly freed Negroes, the abolitionists knew well from their own experience that the rights of white men often needed protection from state governments and unofficial local majorities, *i.e.*, lynch mobs.[20]

In short, the Fourteenth Amendment was intended to destroy the right of any state or individual to deny an individual his "natural rights": it was to be the gravestone of Madisonian federalism. The Amendment was to provide a constitutional foundation for congressional statutes guaranteeing civil rights; indeed, it was the constitutional twin of the great Civil Rights Act of April 9, 1866, which explicitly defined the rights of citizens of the United States and established penalties for "any person who, under color of any law, statute, ordinance, regulation, or *custom*, shall subject, or cause to be subjected, any inhabitant of any State or Territory to the deprivation of any right secured or protected by this act. . . ."[21] [Sec. 2, emphasis added]

Contemporary opinion of the Civil Rights Act and the Fourteenth Amendment has tended to criticism of motivation; they are considered part of a program of conquest and oppression of the South, extremist efforts to destroy the "delicate balance of the federal system." Overlooked in this nostalgia for the "Boys in Gray" is the hard fact that the South went to war for human slavery and the theory of states' rights which buttressed it—and lost. Jefferson Davis and Robert E. Lee may be awarded the Legion of Merit posthumously, but in 1866 they were rebels and traitors, and unsuccessful ones at that. In historical terms, men who launch rebellions play for their heads; Davis, Lee, and the other Confederate leaders were fortunate to escape with their heads intact. But it really is a bit stiff to expect the radical Republicans to have left intact the social system of the South: after four years of bloody conflict, the winners could hardly say "boys will be boys" and pretend that nothing had happened. The Civil Rights Act and the Fourteenth Amendment were designed to destroy the states as effective units of sovereignty and thus make future civil wars impossible. Their technique was the "nationalization" of basic human rights; in essence, the freedom of the individual was withdrawn from the jurisdiction of the states and put under the protection of the national government.

This is not the place for a history of Reconstruction. Suffice it to say that the burning idealism of 1865-66 soon got bogged in the mire of corruption. (The Reconstruction governments of Southern states have been pilloried as the ultimate in boodling, but it is doubtful whether they were any more corrupt than the state governments in the North.) As Professor Woodward has indicated in his perceptive *Reunion and Reaction,* genial President Grant (1868-76) presided over the liquidation of wartime idealism and its replacement by the "great barbecue." [22] The nation, perhaps as a reaction against the demands and tensions of the Civil War, went into an orgy of business and governmental corruption. Forgotten in the festivities were both the ideals of 1866 and the Negro; in 1877, the issue of Negro rights was by general agreement removed from national politics. The unfortunate freedmen were returned to the jurisdiction of state and local governments and there they stayed, in real political terms, until after World War II.

True, the Fourteenth Amendment and various civil rights acts remained on the books, but the Supreme Court undertook by appropriate legal ceremonies to convert these measures into battlefield monuments. Beginning with the *Slaughter-House Cases* (1873), the Court rewrote the Fourteenth Amendment, a process which continued through the *Civil Rights Cases* (1883) to its apotheosis in *Plessy* v. *Ferguson* (1896). By the turn of the century, the Amendment was thoroughly emasculated: it was held only to limit direct state action violating individual liberty, and to permit "separate but equal" treatment of Negroes, *i.e.*, Jim Crow legislation. The great abolitionist dream of nationalized liberty became a nightmare.

To return to the terminology used earlier in this section, the Court replaced the substantive concept of due process of law with a procedural one. The Fourteenth Amendment was held to limit the power of a state to exercise *arbitrary* authority, that is, it forbade "a special rule for a particular person or a particular case" (*Hurtado* v. *California,* 1884). But it did not constitute a check on the scope or substance of state authority. As Justice Miller stated in the *Slaughter-House Cases,* it was inconceivable that the Amendment could be intended to "fetter and degrade the State governments by subjecting them to the control of Congress" or radically to change "the whole theory of the relations of the State and Federal governments to each other." Pristine federalism was thus revived and the years 1860-65 were neatly excised from American constitutional history.

From 1873 until the early 1920's, this was the accepted view of due process in the area of civil rights. However, in a different sector substantive due process achieved respectability and acceptance by the 1890's: the due process clause of the Fourteenth Amendment (and of the Fifth Amendment, which followed in the wake of the Fourteenth) was interpreted to protect property rights from "radical" legislative regulation. In his dissent from the procedural holding in the *Slaughter-House Cases,* Brad-

ley sounded the trumpet which was later to rally a
majority to the defense of "property rights": "In my
view, a law which prohibits a large class of citizens from
adopting a lawful employment, or from following a lawful
employment previously adopted, does deprive them of
liberty as well as property without due process of law.
The right of choice is a portion of their liberty; their
occupation is their property."

In a series of notable dissents, Bradley and his colleague
Justice Stephen J. Field fought manfully for their view.
Field, who was a formidable old pirate, even enforced a
substantive interpretation of both due process and equal
protection of the laws in *his* Ninth Circuit! The cases
in which he did this (which could not be reviewed by
the Supreme Court on technical statutory grounds) illus-
trate, by the way, the degree to which personal liberty and
property rights are so often intermeshed. Field, his Circuit
Judge Sawyer, and his District Judges Deady and Hoffman
in the late 1870's declared war on the anti-Chinese enactments of the West Coast states. While it is true that some
of these statutes and ordinances were cut down because
they infringed the property right of an employer to hire
Chinese workers, in other cases such as the notable
Twenty-One Chinese Prostitutes and the *Queue Case,* Field
and his associates invoked the Fourteenth Amendment to
protect the helpless Chinese from vicious local discrimination. The consequence was, in Graham's words, that
"Chinese aliens on the Pacific coast had rights superior to
American citizens in Louisiana." [23]

But when the Supreme Court in the 1890's got around to
adopting the Bradley-Field gloss on the Fourteenth Amendment, nobody seemed to worry much about Chinese,
Negroes, or other underprivileged minorities. In contrast,
the Court came to the rescue of the business community
which had utilized state power to the maximum in the
quest for riches and power and now discovered that state
governments were moving toward restrictions on their
private sovereignties. The classic American definition of

laissez faire was "Every man for himself—as the elephant said, dancing among the chickens." What has to be recalled is that such elephants as the railroads had achieved their gargantuan status by virtue of public policy, *i.e.*, state and local governments had provided them with franchises, subsidies, and the power of eminent domain and the federal government had supplied huge land grants.[24]

From the 1870's onward, state legislatures, particularly in agrarian sections of the country, began to regulate these "over-mighty subjects" (to borrow a term from Tudor England) and the railroad corporations fought back with every device that superb legal talent could discover or invent. Substantive due process in Bradley's definition was a natural line of defense (though over Bradley's objections: a former railroad counsel, the Justice yet insisted that railroads were quasipublic corporations subject to special legislative control—see his dissent in the *Minnesota Rate Case* [1890]).

At the same time that railroad and corporation lawyers were pressing the case for substantive due process in economic affairs, the Court underwent virtually a total change in composition: of the Justices sitting in 1888, only John Marshall Harlan remained on the bench in 1900. The new members were drawn from circles where Justices Bradley and Field were considered apostles of true constitutionalism so it became only a matter of time before their views became incorporated in the Constitution. At first, in the *Minnesota Rate Case* (1890) and *Smyth* v. *Ames* (1898), the Court's voice was a bit uncertain, but beginning with *Allgeyer* v. *Louisiana* (1897) a note of confidence emerged which reached its peak in the next century.[25]

The vehicle for developing substantive economic process was the concept of "liberty of contract." Essentially adopting a medieval English legal proposition—that a man has a property right in himself—the Court in *Lochner* v. *New York* (1905), *Adair* v. *United States* (1908), *Coppage* v. *Kansas* (1915), and later cases, struck down legislative regulations of the labor market. The assumption underlying these decisions was that, with certain limited exceptions, the individual has a sovereign constitutional right to sell his labor power on his own terms. Thus it became a violation of his personal liberty, guaranteed by the due process clauses of the Fifth and the Fourteenth Amendments, for the national government (*Adair*) or a state government (*Lochner, Coppage*) to dictate to him or to his employer what wages, hours, or conditions of employment can be incorporated in a labor contract.

The unarticulated premise of this doctrine was that there was equality of bargaining power between the individual and the employer. This view, which may have reflected the reality of American life in 1800, supplied little consolation to a sovereign worker told by United States Steel that he could have the privilege of working a sixty-hour week so long as he did not join a trade union, *or* take his liberty of contract with him to the poorhouse. Its innate absurdity, however, did not prevent the Court as late as 1936 (*Morehead* v. *New York ex rel Tipaldo*) from striking down a New York law prescribing minimum wages for women on the ground that it deprived some sturdy, individualistic laundry workers of their right to sell their labor on their own terms.

This is not the place for an elaborate discussion of the economic aspects of due process; for our purposes the important point is that while the Court refused to apply substantive canons to the area of state limitations on civil rights, it did carve out a sector of economic liberty in which substantive criteria were applied to state actions. This set the stage for the next, and most crucial, development: the expansion of the area of protected freedoms to include basic human rights such as freedom of speech, of press, of religion, and of assembly. The principle was in operation, but the scope of the operation awaited expansion.

As late as 1922 (*Prudential Insurance Co.* v. *Cheek*), the Court held that there were no constitutional restraints imposed on the states by the Fourteenth Amendment in

the area of freedom of speech, but in the following year
a curious decision suggested that the Court was moving
in the direction of protecting personal liberty from state
infringement. In this case, *Meyer* v. *Nebraska,* the Court
was asked to rule on a state law which forbade the
teaching of any modern language other than English to
public, private, or parochial grammar school children.
Justice McReynolds declared the statute unconstitutional
as a violation of the due process clause of the Fourteenth
Amendment, but his reasoning was startling: beginning with
standard liberty of contract doctrine (the bill deprived language teachers of their property rights in their subjects!),
McReynolds launched into a full-scale defense of educational freedom, and denounced the state for intruding into
a sector where it had no business to be. Some of this may
be attributed to McReynolds' characteristic choler, but
it did signal the beginning of a new judicial course, a course
which was explicitly affirmed in 1925 (*Gitlow* v. *New
York*) and really implemented for the first time in 1931
(*Near* v. *Minnesota*).

In the Gitlow Case, the Justices agreed that the due
process clause of the Fourteenth Amendment established
the same restrictions on the states that the First Amendment did on the federal government, that is, the substantive rights of speech, press, and opinion were protected
from state invasion to the same extent that the national
government was inhibited by the First Amendment. Judged
by the Court's decisions in wartime and immediate
postwar cases, this was not much of a limitation. Indeed,
Gitlow's conviction for attempting with the aid of an end-
less and soporific manifesto to overthrow the governments
of the United States and New York was upheld by the
Court. Yet the principle was established: the Justices
would exercise oversight on the activities of the states in
limiting First Amendment freedoms.[26]

The *Near Case* marks the real beginning of the modern
tradition: it was the first decision in which state action
was clearly declared unconstitutional because it trans-

gressed personal liberty protected by the due process clause, in this instance freedom of the press from previous censorship. After *Near*, the procession began and in the last thirty years the Supreme Court has ruled on an enormous number of intricate problems in the broad area of freedom of opinion with a view to ascertaining whether a state has gone too far in the direction of restraint. Despite urging from Justice Black and others, the Court has never agreed that the due process clause of the Fourteenth Amendment subjects the states to the identical restraints that the Bill of Rights applies to the federal government. It is clear that the Justices feel that the restrictions of the First Amendment apply to the states *via* due process, but beyond that they have engaged in studied ambiguity. As will be indicated shortly, a state can eliminate grand juries, restrict the right to counsel, even put a man in double jeopardy without violating due process of law—provided the Supreme Court agrees that the individual concerned in any given case has received a "fair trial." Due process in criminal procedure, in other words, requires "fair" actions from the state, and the Justices have vigorously refused to define specifically the nature of "fairness" except in self-validating terms, *i.e.,* a fair trial is one that is not conducted unfairly. This leaves a wide scope for divination and other black arts; indeed, there are those who have suggested that the next appointment to the Court should be a certified *guru* who could provide expert counsel to those Justices whose extrasensory perception leaves something to be desired.

With this as background, let us now turn to an examination of the present status of certain crucial categories of individual and group liberty in the United States. There are a number of possible ways to slice up the data, but for purposes of simplicity I have chosen to deal with the rights themselves, discussing under each heading the degree to which the state and federal governments are affected by the specific limitation under analysis.

Freedom of Speech, Press, Religion, and Assembly

These "First Amendment freedoms" operate with equal force on both state and federal governments. The general rule is that an individual may exercise his freedom in these matters freely up to the point where he constitutes a "clear and present danger" to the community. There is full freedom of opinion so long as it remains only opinion; the instant it becomes a call to action subversive of the goals of society and having a chance of success, restriction may be invoked. In fact, the courts, particularly in a long series of cases brought by Jehovah's Witnesses, have gone a long way with freedom of religion (perhaps reflecting a secular bias that religious opinion is irrelevant to the success or failure of society) and seldom have sustained in the last twenty-five years an attack on the press (perhaps from a healthy respect for the great political potential of the newspaper publishers' lobby). The crucial problems have been freedom of speech and assembly for Communists and, recently, for Southern Negroes.

How does one define a "clear and present danger"? This has been the nub of the problem with regard to the Communists. The libertarian view of the matter is that nothing short of conspiratorial action aimed at seizing power constitutes a clear and present danger; that talk, no matter how flamboyant or incendiary, can never constitute a menace sufficient to justify government action. The conservative view, in contrast, asserts that, in the sharp phrase of the late Justice Jackson, democratic government is not a "suicide pact," that a democracy can and should take action against subversives before they are in a position to launch an insurrection. From this viewpoint, the state is fully justified in intervening to prevent a clear and present danger from developing by clamping down on the subversives before they can get their schemes under way.

Much of the difficulty that Americans have had in making up their minds about this question stems from the nature of the Communist Party, which simply does not fit into the format of earlier radical movements. By contrast with even the militantly radical Industrial Workers of the World, which brought the dream of the "One Big Union" and the "Dictatorship of the Proletariat" to many labor struggles in the early part of this century, the Communist Party has always had a unique and dangerous dimension: its dual apparatus. No "Wobbly" ever went underground—except to dynamite a nonunion mine shaft; he was always proud of his revolutionary mission and was particularly delighted to get an opportunity in a "capitalist court" to express his willingness to overthrow society. The Communist Party, on the other hand, follows rigorously Lenin's instructions to build an underground apparatus separate and distinct from a legal party, an apparatus whose effectiveness depends on its secrecy and lack of identification with the Party's public work. Consequently, when one talks about the Communist Party, he is referring to an organization which is both a legal group expressing in speech and print its anticapitalist opinions *and* an underground movement of unascertained proportions dedicated to revolutionary seizure of power and, above all, to subversive activities on behalf of the Soviet Union.[27]

This was the model of the Communist Party which the United States Department of Justice employed in its Smith Act prosecutions of leading Communist functionaries, and theoretically it was completely sound. No student of the Communist movement, including frank Communists themselves (see, *e.g.,* William Z. Foster's views in *Towards a Soviet America*), would deny that the Party intends to eliminate American capitalistic society at its first opportunity and would employ any weapon necessary for the task. But intentions are one thing and reasonable possibilities something else. On this level it is equally clear that the American Communist Party has been a monumental flop. (Note carefully that I am referring here to the American Communist Party, not the foreign department of the Soviet intelligence system, which is apparently quite efficient.)

In other words, while a good Communist should be willing to be a Soviet spy, all the evidence suggests that the Russians are far too smart to recruit their agents from Party cells, and Soviet agents certainly are not going to wander around atomic energy installations with copies of the *Worker* sticking out of their pockets nor become militants in the Committee to Secure Justice for the Rosenbergs or similar Communist-front organizations. (One may hope that American agents in Russia do not receive their paychecks in the mail nor wave American flags at public functions.) In short, the logical proposition on which the Justice Department built its case (and which was eventually endorsed by the Supreme Court in the *Dennis Case* (1951) sustaining the conviction of the American Communist leadership) was valid, but like most logical propositions somewhat unrealistic in practical application. In postulating the "clear and present danger" rule, Justice Oliver Wendell Holmes noted that no doctrine of free speech could tolerate a man's falsely shouting "Fire!" in a crowded theater, but—to continue the metaphor—it would seem that the American Communists have been shouting "Fire!" in an empty theater and in no real sense constitute a significant menace to the Republic. Moreover, on the basis of recent cases, one may suspect that roughly one Communist in five is a secret member of the Federal Bureau of Investigation; indeed, the F.B.I. may well be the largest financial contributor to the Party!

The real question thus comes down to this: Should we lock up the leaders of the American Communist Party for *intending* to overthrow the government of the United States? Recall that the basis of the Smith Act prosecutions was that the Communists were conspiring to *teach* and *advocate* the violent overthrow of the government and that this teaching and advocating, given the nature of the Party, in itself constituted a "clear and present danger." They were not accused of espionage, sabotage, or even of trying to start an insurrection. Their intentions brought down the wrath of the state, but intentions are a tricky business and the counsels of pragmatism suggest that a wise community avoids exploration of this area, at least until there is some concrete evidence to indicate that intentions are about to be implemented. As Damon Runyon's version of the doctrine of Original Sin put it, every citizen has a touch of larceny in his heart, but, if true, this would hardly justify mass preventative arrests. Running an organized society involves a certain amount of risk-taking, and nowhere is this more important than in the area of free speech. If a nation has that sense of inner security about its goals and methods which Americans should have, it is prepared to ignore patently unrealizable revolutionary intentions. As the British Prime Minister David Lloyd George allegedly told a revolutionist who threatened him with a proletarian dictatorship: "If you try it, I'll call the police."

The Communists have been confronted by formal state action, but the difficulty in the South is on an entirely different level. Whereas the Communists have been tried and convicted under antisubversion statutes, Negro spokesmen in various Southern states, particularly in the deep South, have found themselves prosecuted under a variety of headings. Indeed, seldom does the official record of the case indicate that freedom of speech is involved, a fact that makes review by the Supreme Court extremely hard to obtain. Unlike the prosecutions under the Smith Act, which were major state trials conducted with national publicity, most Southern actions against Negro spokesmen, or "agitators," are harassments with sixty days on the road gang as the typical punishment. These legal actions are designed to discourage "agitation," to point out to the Negro community the disadvantages of heroism, and to take Negro activists out of circulation.

Let us take a hypothetical instance and examine it in some detail; it may give some insight into the meaning of "rights" in a hostile atmosphere where all the institutional dice are loaded against the defendant. A Negro, having read the Supreme Court decision on desegregation, appears

outside a rural Negro school in Alabama and begins to
pass out leaflets to the children, asking them to take the
leaflets home to their parents. The leaflets cite the desegregation opinion and demand an end to segregation in this
school district. As he is passing out the propaganda, he
is arrested by a deputy sheriff for "breach of the peace,"
an ancient catch-all offense at common law. Brought
before a county judge (white) by summary procedures, he is
charged with "breach of the peace" on two specifications:
first, incitement of school children to truancy; and, second,
littering up the public road. He has been privately informed
by the county attorney (white) that if he pleads "guilty,"
he will be let off with a suspended sentence; if not, he will
be "breaking the big rocks and shoveling the little ones"
for sixty days.

What happened to his freedom of speech? Technically,
it is not even at issue in the indictment; inciting children
to play truant and littering up the streets are hardly
exercises in freedom of opinion. On the contrary, they
are clearly "breaches of the peace." And unless the defendant gets himself a good lawyer in a hurry, he would be
better off to plead guilty and retire from politics. In
cases of this sort, the *trial record* is crucial: a skilled counsel introduces the claim of freedom of speech at the outset,
denies the validity of the charges of breaking the peace,
and objects to every aspect of the trial, thus laying the
groundwork for an appeal on constitutional grounds. A
weak lawyer will merely argue that passing leaflets to
children who subsequently threw them on the road was
not, properly speaking, an adequate basis for the charge
of littering the road; he will note the absence of intent to encourage truancy. In contrast, a shrewd civil
rights attorney will demur immediately: he will in effect
say "So what?" and challenge the legality of the charge
itself. And this is vital since the general rule is that appellate
courts will not entertain objections not raised at the trial
level, and appellate courts, including the Supreme Court,
have only the formal record at their disposal.

By now the difficulty should be clear. Unless a Negro "agitator" for equal rights carries a good lawyer around with him, he is likely to wind up on the road gang and there will be nothing that anyone can legally do about it. One major reason why the National Association for the Advancement of Colored People is so unpopular in the South is that it tries to supply counsel in cases such as the hypothetical one described above and thus strikes at the very heart of white hegemony, the effective control of local law enforcement. God is high and the Supreme Court a long way off, but the arrival of a Negro counsel in a small town in rural Alabama to defend a local "agitator" sends shivers up the spines of the magnates and sets them to wondering how long they can maintain their psychological domination over the Negro community if they cannot consign "uppity" troublemakers to sixty days' penance on the roads.

The problems of equal protection of the laws will be discussed later in this chapter; what here concerns us is the difficulty in implementing the right of freedom of speech against a hostile community. There is no such thing as a self-implementing right, and the student of American legal institutions must be constantly aware of the extent to which the exercise of constitutional freedoms depends upon the ability to fulfill certain legal prerequisites. (There are extensive areas in the South where *every* felony conviction of a Negro in the past twenty-five years has properly speaking been unconstitutional because Negroes have been systematically barred from jury panels; yet only a handful of these have been appealed.) The problem is, of course, far broader than the example; the Negro "agitator" has been chosen because this is a matter of enormous contemporary importance, but other minorities have faced the same disabilities in the past and throughout the country. Until the Democratic victory in Philadelphia in 1951, it was standard practice for the police to arrest all sidewalk speakers for breach of the peace, and a soapbox orator still takes his chances in many cities and towns.

The typical policeman takes a dim view of radical activity, has a rather broad definition of radical, and generally views the expression of radical dissent on his beat as a clear instance of "disorderly conduct." As a pacifist, collared by a cop as a Communist for making an anti-H Bomb speech, was told when he protested his *anti*communism: "I don't care what kind of a Communist you are—off you go!"

The reader may find this emphasis on policemen and street corners tedious and wonder what it all has to do with the sacrosanct imperatives of the First Amendment. But the emphasis is deliberate and, I think, correct. For every free speech case that gets litigated, there are probably hundreds which end up as police court convictions for "disorderly conduct" and until Americans realize this and get concerned about it, the situation will continue. To say this is not to deny the importance of Supreme Court rulings on clear and present danger and the rights of Communists; it is merely to emphasize the ironic fact that whatever else may be said about their prosecutions, the Communists always have vigorous lawyers and generally turn every conviction into a legal marathon. We should certainly be concerned about the proper disposition of free speech cases, but we should be even more interested in expanding the scope of the First Amendment protection of freedom of opinion to the legally unprotected, to those without the resources to bring their cases properly before the appropriate forum.

Protection in Criminal Prosecutions

We can rapidly skip over the Second and Third Amendments to the Constitution, although it might be pointed out that the Third, which forbids soldiers being quartered in any house without the owner's consent, has probably been the least violated of the requirements in the Bill of Rights. With the Fourth Amendment, we enter the area of criminal procedures and the Fifth, Sixth, and Eighth deal equally with this matter. Here also we find a significant legal double standard: the Supreme Court has consistently enforced a rigorous doctrine of procedural rights against the federal government, and one considerably less severe against the states. It should perhaps be reiterated that while the Bill of Rights initially limited only the national government, the due process clause of the Fourteenth Amendment has been construed to apply certain provisions as checks on state actions.

To begin with, let us examine the restrictions these amendments put on the procedures of the national government and its officers. The Fourth Amendment covers the area of search and seizure, requiring federal officers to obtain search warrants describing specifically whom, or what, they are in search of. There were to be no general warrants which simply authorized those official fishing expeditions which had so aroused the citizens of Boston when employed by George III's customs inspectors. Technically, the Amendment forbids "unreasonable searches and seizures" and the courts have held that officers in "hot pursuit" of a criminal need not rush off to a judge and obtain a warrant before they can follow the rascal into his home. Similarly a man's automobile has been held not to be his castle, though an interesting case might be raised about house trailers. One of the most intriguing cases of this sort involved the use of a stomach pump by federal agents to retrieve some capsules of heroin hastily swallowed by a California "pusher." Over the furious objections of the Court minority, which pointed out that no other section of the human body enjoyed immunity, the high Court ruled that a man's stomach is indeed protected from summary exploration. The Court has, however, not forbidden the use of blood taken from an unconscious victim of an automobile accident to prove that he was under the influence of alcohol! There is some confusion about the legality of ingenious electronic devices which invade an individual's privacy without actually tapping his wires or otherwise physically invading his premises, but wire tapping is illegal.

Actually, of course, F.B.I. officers, revenue men, Post Office inspectors, and other federal enforcement agents (as those who watch television can verify) do tap wires, quietly search premises, and the like, and it is very difficult, if not impossible, to stop them. For one thing, they generally do so secretly. But what the Fourth Amendment does prohibit with stern rigor is the use of evidence thus obtained in federal prosecutions. This prohibition sometimes operates as an effective check on conviction; Judith Coplon, for instance, was convicted of giving official government information to a Soviet agent on the basis of recorded phone conversations. When the latter were banned by the Court of Appeals and the conviction reversed, the United States had to drop the case for lack of adequate supplementary evidence. More often, information obtained by wire tapping is used to capture a criminal *in flagrante delicto*: he is overheard making an appointment to pick up a package of heroin on the corner of Main and State Streets at six o'clock, and when he arrives and transacts his business, discovers the neighborhood populated with Treasury men, cameramen, sound equipment, and perhaps Howard K. Smith making a C.B.S. crime documentary. There is now no shortage of admissible evidence. Federal officers also cooperate with state law-enforcement agencies, most of whom are not limited by the standards of evidence employed in the federal jurisdiction and will cheerfully pass on information obtained from a bugged house. This evidence can still not itself be introduced in federal court, but it can lead to "red-handed" capture, or to legitimate search and seizure once the federal officers know where to look.

Until June 1961, the Supreme Court permitted the states a wide latitude in employing illegally obtained evidence in criminal prosecutions. However, in *Mapp* v. *Ohio*, the Court suddenly reversed its previous holdings and ruled that all evidence obtained by searches and seizures which would be illegal under federal rules is equally inadmissible in state prosecutions. The due process clause of the Fourteenth Amendment was held to encompass the guarantees of the Fourth Amendment. This surprising reversal by the Court initiated a revolutionary transformation of police behavior in the states.[28]

The Fifth, Sixth, and Eighth Amendments all regulate the conduct of formal criminal prosecutions, requiring indictment by grand jury, forbidding double jeopardy, self-incrimination, excessive bail, cruel and unusual punishments, and insisting on jury trials, confrontation by witnesses, right to counsel, and due process of law. Since each of these, and other ancillary provisions, has been subjected to lengthy analysis by legal historians and Professor David Fellman has written a splendid short study, *The Defendant's Rights*,[29] it would be absurd to attempt here a thorough summation of their implications. To summarize, the Supreme Court has in this area also permitted the states to operate by different standards than does the federal government. In general, the federal courts have been required to maintain far more rigorous procedures than state courts. It should be added that state constitutions and bills of rights may, and sometimes do, establish standards for state judicial proceedings as high as those employed in the federal forum, but a discussion of that problem is beyond our scope. We are here concerned with the extent of federal protection of procedural rights, with the standards which the Supreme Court will enforce willy-nilly on state action.

As far as the Fifth and Sixth Amendments are concerned, the Supreme Court has held that there can be no modification of the indictment by grand jury, the trial by petty jury in serious criminal trials by the national government. While the Constitution did not stop to define grand and petty juries, the Court has held that the meaning of these and of many other similar legal terms must be that subsumed in the common law of Britain, namely, a sixteen to twenty-three man grand jury and a twelve man petty jury. While many state jurisdictions have abolished indictment by grand jury in favor of the more expeditious arraignment by information—in which the state's attorney merely brings a *prima facie,* that is, a seemingly significant and compelling, case to the judge and the latter binds the defendant over for trial—the grand jury is retained for use in all federal prosecutions except misdemeanors. Similarly, some states have modified the size or procedures followed by the trial jury, providing for conviction by two-thirds vote or decreasing its size to eight, but conviction in a federal court (in accordance with a British common law tradition that dates back to 1367) can only follow from unanimous agreement by a jury of twelve. The right to counsel is also enforced with some energy.[30]

It is pointless to go into the details of each provision of these amendments, but it might be worthwhile to examine one provision recently in the news—double jeopardy. The original intention here is clear: no person was to be put twice in jeopardy for the same offense, *i.e.,* tried twice for the identical crime. Technically one is not in jeopardy until the jury is sworn in his case; a mistrial does not result in double jeopardy because until there has been a verdict, jeopardy is not perfected. Once the jury has reached a verdict, jeopardy is however established and the individual cannot again be tried for the identical offense without violating the Constitution—except on his own motion, which is what occurs each time a convicted man appeals a verdict of "guilty" and receives a new trial. In these instances his appeal is treated as a waiver of his rights and it is possible for a defendant who has been convicted of second-degree murder and successfully won a new trial from a Court of Appeals to be convicted of first-degree murder on the second go-round. To make the problem more complex, the same criminal act may involve several violations of the criminal code: a man may be acquitted of breaking into a post office but subsequently convicted of robbing the mails when both acts were committed at the same time.

Moreover, double jeopardy does not prevent two trials for the *identical* offense if they take place in federal and state courts. A number of offenses are punished by both the federal and the state governments and conviction or acquittal in one jurisdiction does not act as a bar on prosecution in the other. This rule was given some notoriety in 1959 when it was affirmed by the Supreme Court in two interesting cases, but it goes back at least to the 1840's and is based on the theory of federalism, of twin sovereignties each with its area of autonomous authority.[31]

To sum up, the individual does not receive due process of law from the federal government if certain procedural rights are not permitted to him. While the exact nature of these procedural guarantees is often a matter of some complexity, nonetheless they can be defined and will be enforced. With regard to the states, the proposition is radically different: the Supreme Court simply refuses to set forth in advance the exact requirements of criminal due process. Instead, it takes each case before it on its individual merits and reaches a determination whether, on the whole record, the individual has received a "fair trial." [32] Sometimes the absence of counsel leads to a decision that the due process required by the Fourteenth Amendment has been denied; other times, the lack of counsel is held not to have prevented a fair trial. And so it goes with all the specific attributes of federal due process. The Court has even held that the clear presence of double jeopardy in a state criminal action did not establish an unfair trial. In other words, every case going up to the high Court within this category presents an essentially metaphysical question to the Justices: was this trial fair? And the Justices fight it out among themselves, leaving behind them no clear lines of precedent to guide state judges and the legal profession.

In addition, this system places a heavy invisible burden

on the defendant and his attorneys. As any lawyer will certify, the crucial point in most appeals is the location of the "burden of persuasion," that is, the designation of the party which has to overcome the presumptions of the court. In federal courts it is pretty clear that when an individual asserts for example that he has been denied counsel, the burden of proof is on the government at the appellate level to show that he was in fact given adequate legal protection. In contrast, when one appeals a state criminal conviction in which the defendant claims to have been denied counsel, the presumption runs the other way: the defendant's lawyers have to demonstrate that the trial was unfair.

The Rights of Negroes

So far we have examined the impact of constitutionally guaranteed rights in the areas of freedom of opinion and criminal procedures; now we turn to what is unquestionably the outstanding issue that Americans today confront—the civil rights of the Negro community, particularly in the states of the deep South. Historically speaking, the Negroes are only the latest in a series of ethnic minorities that have felt the whiplash of majority racial or religious prejudice. However, the situation of the Negro in America is, unfortunately, far more significant today than was the plight of the Irish Catholic in the 1850's or the Chinese-American in the early years of this century. In the first place, there are more Negroes, roughly nineteen million, and in the second place, the status of the Negro in American society has received top billing in international Communist propaganda, notably influential in non-white areas of the world such as Africa and Asia. Rightly or wrongly, when a Negro in Mississippi is lynched, the newspapers in Bombay, Accra, and Cairo consider the event more newsworthy than a billion dollars worth of American aid to these areas. One can complain bitterly that the Communists are dishonest in their claim to have eliminated racial prejudice and point out that in Soviet Russia and its subservient areas anyone will be punished if he asserts the rights of an ethnic or religious minority to autonomy or freedom, but the fact remains that because of our performance in the sector of racial equality we are often judged and found wanting.

It might be wise to point out that foreign views should not determine the content of our Constitution; the fact, for example, that citizens of Burma, or Pakistan, or Monaco, may not like freedom of speech is hardly a justification for eliminating the First Amendment, and the convictions of Mr. Nehru or Mr. Nkrumah do not establish the content of the Fourteenth Amendment. At the same time, we must realize that American professions are constantly contrasted with American practice so that when we announce to the world that the United States stands for the integrity of human personality, there is an immediate rush to discover exactly how our actions conform to our doctrine. And it should be patent, whatever contrary sentiments may emerge from Senators Eastland or Talmadge, that crucial to the American position is the status of the American Negro.

The hard truth is that until recently, the Negro in American society had roughly the legal status of the Jew in medieval Europe. That is to say, he lived at the mercy of the dominant culture and received whatever perquisites the master race chose to bestow. To say this is, oddly enough, not to suggest that Negroes were constantly bullied or maltreated—in fact, most of them minded their own business, avoided trouble, and lived out their lives behind the mask of obsequiousness. This is the unheroic technique of survival, and most human beings have no inclinations to heroic martyrdom. The whites were the master race, they controlled the legal system, the instruments of coercion, the newspapers. It was pointless and futile to challenge this hegemony. The legal codes, and legal decisions, of the South bear witness to this power relationship: if a Negro killed a white man, he was almost automatically executed; if a white man killed a Negro, he might end up for a brief period in jail. In effect, there were two legal universes, one for whites and one for Negroes.

As was pointed out earlier, the radicals of the Civil War period tried to break down this color barrier (the Thirteenth, Fourteenth, and Fifteenth Amendments stand as monuments to their efforts) but for complex political reasons were unsuccessful. In the post-Civil War period, after a brief period of national protection by the Freedmans Bureau and the Army, the Negroes were returned to the control of the white élite in the South and resumed their former dependent status. True, they were no longer slaves, but ingenious labor contracts were devised which in fact gave them most of the disabilities of slavery with few of its advantages. The Supreme Court accepted the situation by agreeing (*Plessy* v. *Ferguson,* 1896) that the Fourteenth Amendment did not require the states to give identical legal standing to whites and Negroes, but rather permitted the establishment of two sets of standards. "Jim Crow" laws, for example, which required the physical separation of the two races in streetcars, theaters, churches, railroad stations, etc., were constitutional—the equal protection clause was interpreted to permit "separate but equal" treatment.

So long as the Negro was a sectional problem, this pragmatic sanction operated with devastating effectiveness. The complete control which white men exercised over local and state governments in the Southern states insured that any Negro who objected to the inferior status of his minority group was dealt with efficiently by the state's "police power." The extent to which this could be carried is demonstrated by the perils of Angelo Herndon, a Negro Communist who tried to organize the "black masses" in the early days of the Depression. Herndon was arrested in Atlanta, Georgia, in 1933 for distributing Communist literature; he was tried and convicted under a state law which was passed well before the Civil War to deal with slave revolts and was sentenced to eighteen to twenty years in prison. Had the jury not recommended mercy, he could have been sentenced to death! Because of the national furor that his case aroused, and the patent horror that this travesty of justice aroused in the decent souls of Chief Justice Hughes and Justice Roberts (who in his decision joined the so-called "liberals" on the bench), the Supreme Court reversed Herndon's conviction five to four. But Herndon was unusually fortunate—he had the vociferous support of the Communists. What about the poor, unaffiliated Negro radical with no friends? [33]

Negro migration out of the South, notably to the big cities of the North, began on a large scale during World War I. Since that time, the Negro has ceased to be a sectional problem and has become an active national concern. No objective observer could suggest for one moment that Northerners, as distinguished from Southerners, were unprejudiced, or that they welcomed the Negro with open arms. On the contrary, the typical reaction was the institution in one form or another of techniques of race prejudice, the Cross which the Negro carried with him wherever he traveled. But there were two major differences between the Southern handling of the Negro and that which he received in the North. First, there was in the North a strong reform current which insisted on the extension of democracy to all Americans, a tradition which went back to the Abolitionist era and which had established an ideal accepted, to a greater or lesser extent, by religious spokesmen, reform journalists, and intellectuals.

Second, and perhaps in the long run equally important, the Negro became a prize in the struggles of practical politicians. In the South, there was after Reconstruction an unwritten agreement among white politicians to bar the Negroes from the political sector. No matter how bitterly they fought among themselves, they stood firm against any efforts to involve the large Negro community in political decisions.[34] This ground rule did not exist in the North, and soon politicians in areas of strong Negro settlement—Harlem, South Philadelphia, Chicago's

South Side—began to compete for Negro support. Soon Negroes in large numbers were being voted (initially they played a passive role in the electoral force) by various machines. The next step, one that successive minorities have taken, was the growth of Negro demands to reward this support. Gradually white politicians began to realize that they had let the demon out of the bottle, that the force which they had begun by manipulating might well end up dominating them. Exactly this has been the fate of both Tammany and the Republicans in New York's Harlem, where white politicians are known as "downtown planters" and their Negro allies as "Uncle Toms."

Roughly half of the nation's Negro population is today outside of the states of the old South and is mainly concentrated in large cities. A majority of the people of the District of Columbia is Negro, a fact which explains the great reluctance of Congress to give the District (which in 1961 received the right to vote in presidential elections) home rule—Southern congressmen with key positions in the national legislature do not appreciate the irony of a possible Negro mayor of Washington. While the Negro vote in the North probably does not hold the "balance of power" between Democrats and Republicans nationally as some Negro spokesmen claim (a diligent political mathematician can probably "prove" that the Kalmucks in Philadelphia hold the "balance of power" if he really puts his back into the effort), it is certainly true that politicians in states with strong Negro minorities must bid for their support. Thus there has developed over the past quarter of a century a significant Negro pressure group, centered around the National Association for the Advancement of Colored People, which fights constantly in public and in private for the rights of the Negro minority. In short, Northern Negroes, armed with that potent weapon, the vote, have become full-scale participants in the national political process.

At the same time, the United States as a whole has

become minority conscious. The war against Nazi Germany required that many Americans rethink their positions on race prejudice, and particularly influenced the views of the political leaders and the opinion leaders. Try today, for example, to find a national magazine of any consequence which does not oppose race prejudice and racial discrimination, and then go back to the files for, say, 1930 and make a comparison. Check also the attitudes of important religious bodies and of the significant trade unions. Whatever other failings we may have picked up in the past generation, it is clear that by contemporary standards race prejudice is in bad odor and that such forms of social pathology as anti-Semitism, anti-Orientalism, and anti-Negro views are on the wane. The great breakthrough clearly came in the immediate post-World War II period: while President Franklin D. Roosevelt obviously detested racism, he equally obviously avoided antagonizing his Southern Democratic magnates by public denunciations of their anti-Negro positions. It was President Harry S. Truman who seized the sword and vigorously struck out at racial discrimination in all government agencies, who desegregated the armed forces, and who split the Democratic Party by his stubborn attitude. Since Truman's time, it has been apparent that racial discrimination in the United States is a violation of national public policy. The Eisenhower and Kennedy administrations have in their characteristic fashions—the former passively, the latter actively—continued and enlarged this program.

The reader at this point may be wondering what this all has to do with the constitutional rights of Negroes. After all, the wording of the equal protection clause of the Fourteenth Amendment has not been altered in the past decade. True, the words of the Constitution are unchanged; but the whole climate within which these words are interpreted has altered. As was suggested earlier, the genius of American constitutionalism is precisely that each generation reads the document afresh and adapts it to the needs of new times and new events. We are living in such a time of adaptation when the courts and other institutions of government, both national and state, are construing the old text in the light of the egalitarian, minority conscious climate of opinion and demanding that racial discrimination be obliterated as a perversion of the democratic ideal.

Due Process of Law and Democratic Fulfillment

In this chapter we have set forth in outline fashion certain historical and contemporary aspects of civil liberties in the United States. The student in search of more detail should consult the many fine legal and institutional studies of special areas that have appeared in recent years; some of the best are cited in the bibliography. Here as elsewhere our material is introductory, but no discussion of civil rights would be complete without some analysis of the function that personal liberty plays in the life and development of a democratic society.

It is important to note that the constitutional protections of personal rights apply to all persons in the United States, not merely to American citizens. According to the terms of the Fourteenth Amendment, all persons born in the United States are citizens of the nation (a microscopic exception exempts the children of foreign diplomatic personnel), and others become members of the community by naturalization. A few born abroad inherit their citizenship from American parents. Most nations in the past limited, and many today still limit, civil rights to their citizens, leaving aliens with only those protections which may have been guaranteed by treaties between the host nation and the nation from which the alien migrated. An alien resident in France, for example, finds himself a special ward of the *Sûreté*, the police, and exercises his vocation at police discretion. In Britain too, the Home Secretary, who supervises police functions, has enormous (though rarely utilized) discretionary power over aliens. In the United States, aliens have roughly the same constitutional standing in vital matters of personal freedom as citizens, and summary procedures are extremely difficult to employ. For example, when the author was a youngster in school, the United States began proceedings to deport Harry Bridges, the alleged Communist leader of the West Coast longshoreman's union. Bridges, however, foiled these efforts, subsequently became a citizen, and still heads his union. In France he would either have been in jail as an undesirable alien or deported twenty years ago.

The constitutional goal, then, is the establishment and maintenance of "due process of law" for all persons in the country, and this due process includes not only such procedural guarantees as the right to jury trial, to counsel, or to refuse to testify against oneself, but also the basic substantive rights to freedom of speech, of press, of assembly, of religion, and to a "fair trial." In short, due process of law is an ideal which governs the subjective content of legal action as well as the objective methods pursued: a seemingly innocent tax on newspapers may be forbidden as a cunning device undermining a free press; an apparently innocuous state law requiring all pressure groups to list their financial supporters may be invalidated as a disingenuous effort to expose to public pressure and infamy those who back unpopular causes.

The basic rationale for this protection is simple. All the procedural guarantees in existence will not protect liberty unless they are part and parcel of a fundamental atmosphere of freedom, an atmosphere in which the individual is free to inform himself, to alter his judgment, and to act on whatever decisions he reaches. To put it another way, the basic postulate of the free society is the absence of any party line, of any mandatory set of policies which must be accepted. Indeed, the free society must even be prepared to accept the freedom of those who oppose its basic premises (within the limits of coercive subversion, of course) and take the calculated risk involved in this dialectic. This is done not because the democrat has blind faith in the truth of his cause, but because he has what David Riesman has termed the "nerve of failure"—the courage to take chances in the full foreknowledge that he may be wrong.

Moreover, his historical insight tells him that every generation produces its status quo, and that nothing is more disastrous for a society than a final victory by any generation and the accompanying establishment of a static set of social and political truths. With Thomas Jefferson, he dreads the tyranny of contemporary truth and holds the perhaps pessimistic conviction that the only thing worse for a community than the wrong kind of change is no change at all. And the mechanism of change as well as its goal (its *telos,* as Aristotle would have said) is due process of law which protects both the personal liberty of the individual and the collective rights of the free community. The constitutional guarantees of civil rights, and the social convictions on which they rest, thus protect this vital process of conflict and establish the rules of the game. While they often seem to operate solely for the benefit of minorities, in fact they are a priceless heritage of the democratic majority.

- 4 -

THE JUDICIARY AND THE
DEMOCRATIC PROCESS

In 1937 President Roosevelt submitted to Congress a proposal (known since as the "Court Packing Bill") temporarily to enlarge the Supreme Court by adding a new
Justice for each of the *six* incumbents over seventy. Much
to the President's surprise and anger this recommendation
set off the most savage political battle of the New Deal
years, one in which he was compared to Hitler and Stalin
and accused of conspiring to destroy the great American
tradition of impartial justice. And what hurt was the impact this line of attack had on the people: despite the
fact that the Supreme Court had invalidated much of the
New Deal, the Democratic voters seemed to join with their
Republican opposites to condemn "tampering" with the
judiciary.

Indeed, the President soon discovered that in public
mythology he was not fighting on behalf of the citizenry
against the antique reactionaries on the high bench. On
the contrary, he was laying profane hands on the Ark of
the Covenant by undermining the Rule of Law. Supreme
Court Justices, so the authorized version ran, were *above
politics* in a legal world sealed off from the turmoil and
prejudice of the political arena. Their task in any specific
litigation was simple; just as the Bureau of Standards
keeps the perfect inch, foot, pound, or pint so that all
and sundry can verify their own measures by an ideal
standard, the Supreme Court guards the perfect Constitu-

tion and employs it to legitimate or void specific acts of national or state governments. For the benefit of readers who may suspect exaggeration in this formulation, let me quote from Justice Roberts' decision for the Court striking down the Agricultural Adjustment Act of 1933:

> "There should be no misunderstanding as to the function of this court in such a case. It is sometimes said that the court assumes a power to overrule or control the action of the people's representatives. This is a misconception. The Constitution is the supreme law of the land . . . and legislation must conform to the principles it lays down. When an act of Congress is appropriately challenged [the Supreme Court] has only one duty—to lay the article of the Constitution which is invoked beside the statute which is challenged and to decide whether the latter squares with the former. . . . This court neither approves nor condemns any legislative policy. Its delicate and difficult office is to ascertain and declare whether the legislation is in accordance with, or in contravention of, the provisions of the Constitution; and, having done that, its duty ends. . . ." (*United States* v. *Butler,* 1936)

The attack on Roosevelt was brilliantly managed, with Chief Justice Charles E. Hughes organizing the nonpolitical Justices in a superb nonpolitical defense of their role. At the same time, the Court seems to have taken a fresh (and, of course, nonpolitical) look at some of the Constitution's objective requirements: the Wagner National Labor Relations Act was held up against the commerce power by the Chief Justice and found to fit. Like General Douglas MacArthur, Hughes never retreated—he firmly advanced to the rear, sowing the countryside with legal land mines as he went (*Jones & Laughlin Steel Co.* v. *N.L.R.B.,* 1937). In short, the Court took evasive action and thus undermined the President's case. (In neither *Jones & Laughlin* nor *West Coast Hotel* v. *Parrish,* 1937, which sustained the state of Washington's minimum wage law for women, did Hughes *overrule* previous anti-New Deal decisions. He neatly stepped around them!) Hughes demonstrated by this the talent which was wasted when

Wilson defeated him for President in 1916; he was the one man in the New Deal years who took President Roosevelt to the mat and won.[1]

What concerns us here are not the intricacies of the Court fight, but the issues involved and the reaction of the press and the people to this attempted exercise of an undoubted congressional power, that of determining the size of the Supreme Court. Roosevelt, it should be recalled, had just defeated Landon by an Electoral College majority that will probably stand uniquely for the rest of time: the Republican candidate in 1936 received the votes of Maine and Vermont! Therefore when Roosevelt in February of 1937 turned his attention to the "horse and buggy" judiciary which had been sabotaging the New Deal program with savage dedication (at one time shortly after the Wagner Act became operative, there were over a hundred injunctions simultaneously in effect against the Labor Board!), one might logically presume that his assault would be overpowering. Instead the outcome was a political shambles. Why?

First of all, it has to be admitted that Roosevelt played his hand badly and that Hughes played his with consummate skill. But while these subjective considerations undoubtedly played a part in the unfolding of events, they are insufficient to explain the strong position held by the judges in the American system of government. The underlying buttress of judicial power is the fragmentation of political power and the absence of strong, national political parties. This is equally the case in situations adjudged "good" and those considered "bad." It was the same absence of responsibility (in the technical sense, not the personal; the most personally responsible judges are still irresponsible in that they operate free from public checks) which made it possible for a federal judge ("conservative") to void the N.R.A. *and* for a federal judge ("liberal") to invalidate anti-Communist excesses.

Return for a moment to President Roosevelt's encounter with the Court in the spring of 1937. On the face of it, he had received an enormous vote of confidence in 1936: in the House, the Democrats had control (331-89), and in the Senate, 16 Republicans held on desperately against 76 Democrats and their 4 progressive or farm labor allies. Yet the Democrats were anything but united and, if anything, the size of the majorities encouraged factionalism and loose discipline. In particular, the Southern Democrats, who then as now held firmly to the commanding heights of congressional power, the committee chairmanships, were muttering and caballing against the "radicalism" of their Northern Democratic colleagues, especially the militants of the labor movement.

In other words, the 331 Democrats in the House of Representatives were not a unified body, but a congeries of bodies representing different policy orientations ranging from crypto-Communist at one extreme to proto-Fascist at the other. But House party discipline was still better than that in the Senate (which traditionally resents the whip) where powerful committee chairmen openly declared war on Roosevelt. The Republicans in both houses were thus in the happy position of spectators at a free-for-all Democratic squabble—and their leaders, in order further to encourage the Democratic imbroglio, instructed the G.O.P. remnant virtually to play dead. For example, the Republican Senate leaders agreed not to intervene in the Court fight as a body—this might rally the discordant Democrats —but to give individual assistance to the anti-F.D.R. Democrats when requested, and to vote for Democratic pro-Court motions rather than introducing their own.[2]

Had the Democrats in Congress constituted a "parliamentary party" in the British sense, i.e., a group of representatives under discipline and with a high level of policy cohesion, the outcome would have been different. Indeed, if we had the British political system, we might be much happier all round—or, as those commentators who look wistfully toward Westminster often forget, we might resemble the Third and Fourth French Republics, which "had" the British political system. In any case, the ab-

sence of strong national political parties in the United
States is not due to any mechanical deficiencies. On the
contrary, it is a reflection of the size, differentiation, and
diffusion of power which happens to constitute the American facts of life.[3]

This vacuum in the power to govern which arises from
the internal conflicts in Congress, in the parties, and even
in the executive (Was John F. Kennedy elected as a
"liberal"?) leaves the judiciary with great maneuverability
and flexible jurisdiction. Let us examine in some detail the
background of this judicial authority with specific reference
to school desegregation, the crucial domestic issue of the
hour. The remarks that follow are directly pointed to the
institutional questions; it should be obvious to the reader
by now where my sympathies lie in the substantive problem.

The United States, a bold leader in so many areas of
human knowledge, was cursed from the outset with the race
problem. Paradoxically the nation which had made the
terms equality and freedom more meaningful for its white
citizens than any other country in history was the last
important Western power (Brazil possibly excepted) to
abolish human slavery. By 1950 the successor institutions
to slavery, described in some detail earlier in this book,
were a moral disgrace in terms of the democratic ethic
and were a practical liability in the world-wide contest with
the Soviet Union. The United States could hardly pose as
the defender of freedom with a Constitution that authorized
white supremacy and Jim Crow laws. The Soviets, despite
their totalitarian record, escaped from this obloquy, perhaps because, to use a clever phrase of William F.
Buckley's, they employ an F.E.P.C. approach to persecu-
tion: they subjugate without reference to race, color, or
creed.

Thus in the United States two attacks on racial discrimination merged in the post-World War II period: the moral
and the pragmatic. But, there was a great problem:
Where to put the lever? President Truman did what he
could within his range of administrative authority, de-

segregating the armed forces and government facilities, but the real problem was not national in origin. Racial discrimination was almost wholly based on state laws which had by implication received constitutional endorsement. And the white supremacists who ruled these states were unmoved by either moral or pragmatic pleas; they rested immobile behind the barricade of states' rights.

Their constitutional complacency was rudely shattered by the Supreme Court's 1954 decision that state laws segregating students in public schools were a violation of the Fourteenth Amendment. While the Court confined its opinion to education, the logic on which it rested imperiled the whole edifice of racial segregation under public auspices. (It should be recalled that *Plessy* v. *Ferguson* (1896) dealt *only* with segregation in transportation, but was soon justifying the whole corpus of Jim Crow legislation.) The Supreme Court, which Southern politicians had in fine conservative phraseology defended so passionately from Roosevelt's clutches in 1937, now became a prime target. Those who had been opponents of the Court in 1937 also swapped weapons; liberal law professors began to talk like Edmund Burke about the beauties of tradition.[4]

The Supreme Court had done its work. The Fourteenth Amendment's Section 1 was interpreted to forbid racial discrimination in public education. Now in any rational scheme of things the burden would pass to the legislature, which according to Section 5 of the Amendment has the power to implement Section 1. Congress, in other words, could pass a Civil Rights Act which made it a federal offense for anyone to attempt to enforce segregation in the schools. It was in roughly this fashion that the national government destroyed polygamy in Utah seventy-five years ago.[5] Once the Supreme Court held that polygamy was not a legitimate exercise of freedom of religion, the Mormons were at the mercy of federal legislation.

To state the problem this baldly is to emphasize the impossibility under current conditions of Congress really drawing the sword against the Southern states. Let us examine briefly the Senate of the 87th Congress which convened in January 1961. Almost the first matter before the Senate was the alteration of Rule 22 which makes it virtually impossible to block a filibuster; a combination of Republicans and Southern Democrats blocked any amelioration. Then committee chairmanships were assigned on the basis of seniority with the following results:

Committee	*Chairman*	*State*
Aeronautical & Space	Kerr	Oklahoma
Agriculture	Ellender	Louisiana
Appropriations	Hayden	Arizona
Armed Services	Russell	Georgia
Banking & Currency	Robertson	Virginia
District of Columbia	Bible	Nevada
Finance	Byrd	Virginia
Foreign Relations	Fulbright	Arkansas
Government Operations	McClellan	Arkansas
Interior	Anderson	New Mexico
Interstate & Foreign Comm.	Magnuson	Washington
Judiciary	Eastland	Mississippi
Labor & Public Welfare	Hill	Alabama
Post Office & Civil Serv.	Johnston	South Carolina
Public Works	Chavez	New Mexico
Rules & Administration	Mansfield	Montana
Small Business	Sparkman	Alabama

The reader who sat up all election night nervously watching Ohio, New Jersey, Michigan, Illinois, or California will immediately notice the eccentric character of this roster. Alabama, Arkansas, New Mexico, and Virginia each have two chairmen, but where are the chairmen from the big urban states? There are none, and while the situation in the House is better, even in the lower chamber they are few. Power in Congress thus accrues to Representatives from one-party districts and to Senators from one-party states. In the event the reader feels this is a special problem for the Democrats, let me construct the same roster as it would probably appear had the Republicans captured the Senate:[6]

Committee	Chairman	State
Aeronautical & Space	Smith	Maine
Agriculture	Aiken	Vermont
Appropriations	Bridges	New Hampshire
Armed Services	Saltonstall	Massachusetts
Banking & Currency	Capehart	Indiana
District of Columbia	Beall	Maryland
Finance	Williams	Delaware
Foreign Relations	Wiley	Wisconsin
Government Operations	Mundt	South Dakota
Interior	Dworshak	Idaho
Interstate & Foreign Comm.	Schoeppel	Kansas
Judiciary	Dirksen	Illinois
Labor & Public Welfare	Goldwater	Arizona
Post Office & Civil Serv.	Carlson	Kansas
Public Works	Case	South Dakota
Rules	Curtis	Nebraska
Small Business	Javits	New York

Illinois and New York are at least represented on this list, but again the urban states, considering their contribution to any election victory, are grievously shortchanged.

A further relevant dimension emerges when one asks the next question: What areas of the nation are "minority conscious," are in the forefront in the struggle for racial equality? They are, of course, precisely the states in which politics is a competitive dynamic affair, in which a Senator is lucky to last three terms before the opposition catches up with him—in which, in sum, Senators have great difficulty accumulating that seniority which is the key to power in the Senate. In the effort to amend Rule 22 in January 1961, an interesting and not uncommon voting pattern emerged. On the same, "liberal" side of this particular vote were found: two Republicans from New York, one Republican and one Democrat from California, one Republican and one Democrat from Pennsylvania, two Democrats from Ohio, one Democrat and one Republican from New Jersey, two Democrats from Michigan, and the Democrat from Illinois. The only Senators from big industrial states who voted on the other, "drop-the-problem" side were the two Democrats from Texas and the Republican from Illinois. And it should be added that the vote referred to here dealt with a proposal to decrease the majority required for shutting off debate from two-thirds to three-fifths!

With presidential authority limited and Congress under the control of men either opposed or indifferent to the implementation of the Court's decision, the whole burden has fallen upon the judicial system. The Supreme Court has in fact become a national school board with the fearful task of attempting by judicial decrees to reorganize local institutions in the Southern states. This is inherently absurd, not because the Court does not have the *authority* under the Constitution to lay down the law to the states (it does) but because courts are simply not designed as administrative agencies. When a federal District Judge orders compliance with a bankruptcy decree, he is in his element. When he orders the New Orleans School Board to disobey the Louisiana Legislature and desegregate public schools, he is suddenly wandering alone in a strange universe. From a political viewpoint, his crucial weakness is his lack of the power of initiative; he must sit quietly while the opposition devises gimmick after gimmick to evade a decision, and only after litigation comes officially before him, can he exercise his authority.

When, as in New Orleans in the winter and spring of 1960-61, the segregationists have firm control of the state legislature and a stable full of ingenious lawyers, the judicial process begins to resemble a tennis match, with the federal judge always on the defensive, batting back new attempts to circumvent his ruling and then waiting for the next smash. And while this ritualized legal game of wits is going on, the extra-legal sanctions—which the judge cannot touch—are making a mockery of his courage and perseverance. What can he do if a white garage mechanic who sends his child to a desegregated school is intimidated by mobs, fired from his job, and finally moves back to his old home in Rhode Island? No one has a constitutional obligation to be a hero, much less to make heroes of his small children. What can the judge do when pickets appear outside a drug store, exercising their freedom of opinion, and convince the drug firm to transfer a white man who has sent his children to school with Negroes to another location? What can he do when local banks and merchants, themselves often under severe pressure, cut off credit to those who cooperate in desegregation?

To say this is not to criticize the work of the courts, which have done surprisingly well given their functional limitations, but to point out the anomalous character of "government by lawsuit" in a vital area of public policy. This is particularly true when one realizes that federal District judges are local political figures and are often reluctant warriors: action did not begin in Little Rock, Arkansas, until a "foreign" District judge from the North appeared temporarily to fill the post, and the District judge in New Orleans had to be stimulated to confront the legislature by the Court of Appeals. My fundamental point is that the federal judiciary is not properly designed either in theory or in practice to undertake policy decisions. Sometimes by innate conviction, as in the judicial crusade against the New Deal, and sometimes by the inexorable determination of the Supreme Court motivated by both expediential and principled considerations, the courts march into a policy battleground.

In political terms this can be justified by necessity, by the existence of an area where for one reason or another the national government refuses to exercise necessary jurisdiction through its elected officials. In practical terms we can understand why it happens: the inability of our party system to supply a unified package of leadership and policy which leaves whole sectors of national life in a contested no-man's-land. Like the General who observed of World War II that it was a second-rate war, but better than no war at all, we can accept as a necessary evil judicial determination of policy in these twilight zones. Finally, as students of history we must recognize that under no system can the judge be wholly excluded from dabbling in policy: the old dream of Jeremy Bentham and the Utilitarians that the law could be set forth by the legislature in unambiguous terms so that the judicial function would become superfluous is a practical impossibility. Even in France, where all judicial decisions are collective and anonymous and the Code supposedly rules, the subjective views of judges on occasion intrude in policy matters.

But having admitted all this on the practical, operational level, we have still not faced up to the underlying issue. And by these admissions, we should not be understood to have waived the right to argue the principle. While there is obviously very little principled analysis of the role of the courts in the political sector, students of political science have to be concerned with the ideal as well as with the realities. We can suggest, for example, that when Senator James Eastland of Mississippi observed in 1955 that the Supreme Court had been "brainwashed," he was reacting viscerally to the desegregation decision and not directing himself to the principle of judicial review. When Eastland said "the Court has not only arrogated to itself powers which were not delegated to it under the Constitution [but] they are attempting to graft into the organic law of the land the teachings, preachings, and social doctrines [of] Karl Marx," [7] he overlooked the fact that in 1896 the Supreme Court put Jim Crow *into* the Constitution on the basis of contemporary racist dogmas. The fundamental question which Eastland begged was: what right did the Court have either to constitutionalize *or* to void Jim Crow?

I am not suggesting for a minute that in this contingent world we should fight the good in the name of the perfect and thus fall prey to the paralysis of perfectionism. As citizens and realists we may rejoice in "good" Supreme Court decisions and denounce "bad" ones, but at the same time we should in our analytical capacities be aware of the fact that there is no sound justification for judicial policy-making. Essentially it is a Platonic graft on the democratic process—a group of wise men insulated from the people have the task of injecting truth serum into the body politic, of acting as an institutional chaperone to insure that the sovereign populace and its elected representatives do not act unwisely.

In other words, one is free to reject the democratic premise that the people, through their elected spokesmen, are capable of self-government, but he should be aware of his élitism and its implications. Thus one could defend the legislative sabotage of the Democratic congressional program by the House Rules Committee (even after it was partially *un*packed in January 1961), the Senate filibuster, or the practice of gerrymandering on the old medieval-Aristotelian ground that some votes are more valuable than others. John C. Calhoun developed this thesis at length in his *Disquisition on Government,* praising what he called "concurrence," and denouncing the majority principle. Senator Harry F. Byrd, Chairman of the Senate Finance Committee, today echoes Calhoun when, in obstructing federal spending programs, he claims that a majority can always be rallied for giveaway enactments. The people, in short, must be defended not only against external enemies, but against their own Original Sin which, unfettered by counsels of restraint, would lead them to destruction. In a curious way Senators like Byrd, Goldwater, and Williams, and Representatives like Howard W. Smith and John Taber have set themselves up as spokesmen for a Rousseauistic "general will." They believe and assert that they are protecting the *real* "national interest"—that corpus of policies which are *really* in the best interests of the people of the United States. And before the reader mutters a ritual curse against "reactionary standpatters," he should search his own soul to insure that his ideal society is not one in which *he,* and sound, like-minded associates, exercise Byrd's functions.

If one rejects, as I do, the proposition that the people have to be protected from themselves, it is not from dreamy optimism nor from any mystical faith in the infallibility of public opinion. On the contrary, the essence of my defense of democracy is that it is the one system devised to date premised on the manifest *fallibility* of man, the one system which asserts that all men and women (not just nobles, rich men, or Party members) are full members of the community entitled to a say in its destinies. Thus the leaders must look for public sanction and the people always retain the right to reject one set in favor of another. This may on occasion lead to demagoguery, "father images," and sheer incompetence, but the alternative is a frozen, self-validating, and inevitably dictatorial system. As Winston Churchill once observed in a moment of pessimism, "democracy is the worst system ever invented—except for all the rest."

In conclusion, the current policy power of the federal judiciary is an anomaly in our democratic system. The judiciary rightfully has a strong and vital role to play in society: to insure that the "principles of natural justice" are enforced in litigation, that citizens are not victimized by arbitrary and capricious government procedures, and, of course, that appropriate legal norms are applied in litigation between private parties. But it is not the function of judges to determine social and economic policy: their task is to apply those policies decided upon by the responsible organs of government to cases at bar. Perhaps this can best be summarized in the words of a federal District judge who recently was confronted by a conflict between the provisions of two federal statutes. Asked to rule on whether a provision of the Taft-Hartley Act had implicitly overruled a section of the Norris-La Guardia Act, Judge Wright announced that even if he "read the weather vane as indicating a judicial overruling of the Norris-La Guardia Act [and] thought that solution desirable, [the Court] could not presume to ignore the plain mandate of applicable statute in order to achieve a result in accord with its private view of what the law ought to be. Perhaps that privilege belongs to a higher court. Or perhaps Congress itself should be permitted to do its own legislating." [8] Perhaps Congress should?

NOTES AND REFERENCES

1. THE RULE OF LAW

1. The best introduction to early Western political theory is still Charles H. McIlwain, *The Growth of Political Thought in the West* (New York, 1932).

2. The whole problem of tyrannicide, which is the problem of legitimacy stood on its head, is carefully examined in Oscar Jaszi and John D. Lewis, *Against the Tyrant* (Glencoe, Ill., 1957).

3. See A. P. D'Entrèves (ed.), *Aquinas: Selected Political Writings* (Oxford, 1948); F. C. Copleston, *Aquinas* (London, 1955).

4. A superb antidote to the common view that Plato and Aristotle were *the* Greek philosophers is Eric A. Havelock, *The Liberal Temper in Greek Politics* (New Haven, 1957).

5. The classic study of the opportunistic character of this theory is John N. Figgis, *The Divine Right of Kings* (Cambridge, 1914); a recent and masterly analysis of the open-ended aspect of the theory is E. H. Kantorowicz, *The King's Two Bodies* (Princeton, 1957).

6. See R. W. and A. J. Carlyle, *A History of Mediaeval Political Theory in the West,* Vol. I, pp. 33-79 (Edinburgh & London, 1950).

7. *Ibid.,* p. 170 (my paraphrase).

8. D'Entrèves, *op. cit.,* p. 183.

9. Pp. 141-194 (Boston, 1960).

10. *Religion and the Rise of Capitalism* (New York, 1926).

11. The best analysis of the varying Protestant political theories for the general reader is J. W. Allen, *A History of Political Thought in the Sixteenth Century* (London, 1928).

12. Quoted by C. V. Wedgewood in her incisive *The Thirty Years War* (London [Pelican ed.], 1957), p. 42.

13. See George Gooch and Harold Laski, *English Democratic Ideas in the Seventeenth Century* (London, 1927), p. 19.

14. Wolin, *op. cit.,* Chapter 8, is extremely perceptive on Hobbes. He has avoided the pitfall of overestimating Hobbes' logical compulsion which has led some commentators into esoteric quagmires. Hobbes was quite capable of rising above logical consistency in the interest of scoring a good point. Richard Peters, *Hobbes* (London, 1956) is a lucid philosophical exposition of Hobbes' overall system.

15. The *Second Treatise* requires careful reading: what Locke gives away at one point, he retrieves at another. Most commentators seem to overlook the critical institutional connotations of Section 119 in which Locke explicates his theory of "tacit consent." I generally share Willmoore Kendall's view that Locke was an exponent of majority rule rather than of vested rights, cf. Kendall, *John Locke and the Doctrine of Majority Rule* (Urbana, Ill., 1941).

16. See J. W. Gough (ed.), *The Second Treatise of Civil Government and A Letter Concerning Toleration* (Oxford, 1948), pp. 154, 156. Locke essentially endorsed religious freedom for religious people.

17. This whole dispute is chronicled in a masterly way by Clinton L. Rossiter, *Seedtime of the Republic* (New York, 1953). Carl Becker's valuable *Declaration of Independence* (New York, 1922) has to be treated cautiously. In the first place, Becker considered Locke to be the *legitimate* father of American revolutionary theory; in the second, he injected an architectonic principle into the chaos of the years

1763-1776 and thus imposed a deceptive symmetry on events which were in fact disorganized.

18. See Sir Lewis Namier, *The Structure of British Politics at the Accession of George III* (London, 1929), and *England in the Age of the American Revolution* (London, 1930).

19. See John P. Roche, "American Liberty," in Milton Konvitz and Clinton Rossiter (eds.), *Aspects of Liberty* (Ithaca, N.Y., 1958).

20. See Charles Fairman, "The Supreme Court and the Constitutional Limitations on State Governmental Authority," *University of Chicago Law Review,* Vol. XXI, pp. 40-78 (1953).

21. See Roche, *op. cit.,* pp. 140-145.

2. THE JUDICIAL PROCESS

1. 9 *Hening's Statutes* (Va.) 127.

2. Charles Warren, *The Making of the Constitution* (Boston, 1928) is the best introduction to the work of the Constitutional Convention.

3. On the history and function of the Supreme Court see Charles Warren, *The Supreme Court in United States History* (Boston, 1947), and Felix Frankfurter and James M. Landis, *The Business of the Supreme Court* (Boston, 1927).

4. Quoted in Warren, *The Supreme Court in United States History* [2 vol. ed.], Vol. I, p. 34.

5. Charles P. Smith, *James Wilson* (Chapel Hill, 1956), pp. 376-388.

6. 1 *U.S. Statutes at Large* 73.

7. For an authoritative and fascinating study of the crisis of 1798-1800 see James M. Smith, *Freedom's Fetters: The Alien and Sedition Laws and American Civil Liberties* (Ithaca, N.Y., 1956).

8. The best study of Marshall's sleight of hand in the Marbury case is in Edward S. Corwin, *The Doctrine of Judicial*

Review (New York, 1914). There is no reason to believe that Section 13 was intended to enlarge the original jurisdiction of the Court. It merely provided that where the Court had jurisdiction, it could issue certain writs to implement and supplement its existing authority.

9. Every student of American history and politics should read what is, in my view, the finest chronicle ever written by an American historian: Henry Adams, *A History of the United States during the Administrations of Jefferson and Madison* (New York, 1889-1891). It can be found in an excellent abridgement by Herbert Agar (ed.), *The Formative Years*, 2 vols. (London, 1948). The quotation is from p. 194 of this edition.

10. Quoted by Alpheus T. Mason, *The Supreme Court from Taft to Warren* (Baton Rouge, 1958), p. vii.

11. See John P. Roche, "Judicial Self-Restraint," *American Political Science Review*, Vol. XLIX, pp. 762-777 (1955).

12. Senator Dirksen was quoted in *The New York Times*, March 3, 1961; Senator Russell in *Congressional Quarterly*, 1961, p. 385 (March 10, 1961).

13. See Warren, *op. cit.*, Vol. I, Chapter 3.

14. *Ibid.*, Vol. II, pp. 10-11.

15. See Mason, *op. cit.*, pp. 66, 69; Henry F. Pringle, *The Life and Times of William Howard Taft* (New York, 1939), Vol. II, p. 967.

16. See Frankfurter and Landis, *op. cit., passim.*

17. Generally on procedure see the comprehensive treatise by Richard F. Robertson and Francis R. Kirkham, in Wolfson and Kurland (eds.), *Jurisdiction of the Supreme Court of the United States* (New York and Albany, 1951).

18. Refusal to grant certiorari does not in theory imply any agreement with the decision below, though in fact, of course, it sustains the holding. See Justice Frankfurter's lecture in *Baltimore Radio Show* v. *Maryland*, cert. den., 338 U.S. 912 (1950).

19. See John P. Frank, "Political Questions," in Edmond Cahn (ed.), *Supreme Court and Supreme Law* (Blooming-

ton, Ind., 1954). In 1960, it began to appear that the Court might be in the process of reëxamining its view that gerrymandering is a "political question" beyond judicial remedy. In *Gomillion* v. *Lightfoot,* 81 S. Ct. 125, _____ U.S. _____ (1960), a unanimous Court, speaking through Justice Frankfurter (who was responsible for the judgment of the Court in *Colegrove* v. *Green*) held that an Alabama statute redefining the city limits of Tuskegee was a violation of the Equal Protection Clause of the Fourteenth Amendment. It was, the Court held, a thinly disguised piece of racial discrimination designed to remove from the city's voting roll all but four or five of four hundred Negro voters while not excising a single white voter. Although this decision dealt specifically with a racial gerrymander, it would be difficult to support logically the proposition that racial minorities *alone* are protected from gerrymandering. Perhaps realizing this, the Court subsequently heard argument on two gerrymandering cases where the racial issue was absent, but put off decision until the 1961-2 Term in Court.

20. See Robert E. Cushman, *The Independent Regulatory Commissions* (New York, 1941).

21. He must answer. See *Wilson* v. *United States,* 221 U.S. 361 (1911); *United States* v. *White,* 322 U.S. 694 (1944).

22. They can be deducted. See *Commissioner of Internal Revenue* v. *Sullivan,* 356 U.S. 27 (1958).

3. THE RIGHTS OF THE CITIZEN

1. This motif permeated his whole body of historical writing. For an excellent selection of articles see Helen M. Cam (ed.), *Selected Historical Essays of F. W. Maitland* (Cambridge, 1957).

2. William Stubbs (ed.), *Select Charters,* 8th ed. (Oxford, 1905), p. 85.

3. Sir William Holdsworth, *A History of English Law,* 7th ed., revised (London, 1956), pp. 312-350.

4. There is an excellent historical treatment of the law of seditious libel in Leonard W. Levy, *Legacy of Suppression* (Cambridge, 1960), pp. 88-175.

5. See Felix Rackow, "The Right to Counsel: English and American Precedents," *William and Mary Quarterly,* 2d series, Vol. XI, pp. 3-27 (1954).

6. Which is not to say that torture was not used in England. It was, but not at common law. In state trials for treason, or other political and religious offenses of a serious character, a prerogative writ could be obtained from the Crown authorizing torture and the evidence thus obtained was used in prosecutions before the Council or the Star Chamber, which were not common law courts. Litigious political prisoners often demanded to see the writ before they would submit to the rack; Jesuits in particular insisted that the Latin in the writ be letter-perfect.

7. *Poor* v. *Green.* Cited by Richard Morris, *Studies in the History of American Law* (New York, 1930), pp. 12-13.

8. *Ibid.,* pp. 41-46.

9. Rossiter, *op. cit.,* has developed this thesis fully and lucidly.

10. Cited by Julius Goebel, Jr., *Cases and Materials on the Development of Legal Institutions* (New York, 1946), p. 278.

11. Cited in Willard Hurst, "Treason in the United States," *Harvard Law Review,* Vol. LVIII, p. 267 (1944).

12. Levy, *op. cit.,* Chapters 5 and 6.

13. *Ibid.,* pp. 262 ff.

14. In *The People Yes* (New York, 1936).

15. See Roche, "American Liberty," *op. cit.,* for an elaboration of this thesis.

16. See Russel B. Nye, *Fettered Freedom: Civil Liberties and the Slavery Controversy* (East Lansing, Mich., 1949).

17. See Jacobus ten Broek, *The Anti-Slavery Origins of the Fourteenth Amendment* (Berkeley, 1951); Howard Jay

Graham, "The Early Anti-Slavery Backgrounds of the Fourteenth Amendment," *Wisconsin Law Review,* Vol. 1950, pp. 479-507, 610-661 (1950); John P. Frank and Robert F. Munro, "The Original Understanding of 'Equal Protection of the Laws,'" *Columbia Law Review,* Vol. L, pp. 131-169 (1950).

18. Cited in Nye, *op. cit.*

19. Graham, "Our 'Declaratory' Fourteenth Amendment," *Stanford Law Review,* Vol. VII, pp. 3-39 (1954); "Procedure to Substance—Extra-Judicial Rise of Due Process, 1830-1860," *California Law Review,* Vol. XL, pp. 483-500 (1953); and the articles cited in note 17 above.

20. This is sharply delineated in the fine study by Eric McKitrick, *Andrew Johnson and Reconstruction* (Chicago, 1960).

21. 14 *U.S. Statutes at Large* 27.

22. C. Vann Woodward, *Reunion and Reaction* (Boston, 1951); see also his great work *The Origins of the New South* (Baton Rouge, 1951).

23. For an examination of this intriguing episode in judicial feudalism see Howard Jay Graham, "Justice Field and the Fourteenth Amendment," *Yale Law Review,* Vol. LII, pp. 851-889 (1943).

24. See Carter Goodrich, *Government Promotion of American Canals and Railroads, 1800-1890* (New York, 1960).

25. An excellent summary of the development of the Fourteenth Amendment is Edward S. Corwin, *Liberty Against Government* (Baton Rouge, 1948).

26. The classic volume in this area is Zechariah Chafee, Jr., *Free Speech in the United States* (Cambridge, 1946).

27. A good general study is Irving Howe and Lewis Coser, *The American Communist Party* (Boston, 1957); Theodore Draper is doing the definitive history of the Party, two volumes of which have appeared: *The Roots of American Communism* (New York, 1957), and *American Communism and Soviet Russia* (New York, 1960).

28. For a discussion of some of the problems involved see

J. A. C. Grant, "The Tarnished Silver Platter: Federalism and Admissibility of Illegally Seized Evidence," *U.C.L.A. Law Review,* Vol. VIII, pp. 1-43 (1961). After drifting along for years without significant alteration, the problem of illegally obtained evidence received dramatic handling by the Court in the 1959 and 1960 terms. In 1959, the Justices destroyed the so-called "silver platter" doctrine by ruling that illegally obtained evidence could not be admitted in federal criminal trials even when federal officials had no hand in the procurement. *Elkins* v. *United States,* 364 U.S. 209 (1960). This completely closed the federal jurisdiction to evidence procured in violation of the Fourth Amendment (assuming that defense counsel raise timely objection to the introduction of evidence so procured), but left the states in a position where (under the holding in *Wolf* v. *Colorado,* 338 U.S. 25, 1949) they could employ evidence which had been obtained in violation of the Constitution. This decision was seemingly based on the view that although the Fourth Amendment limited the states via the Due Process Clause of the Fourteenth Amendment, this limitation was ethereal: the Court told the states they *should* not use tainted evidence, but did not concretely circumscribe state rules of evidence. Abruptly in June, 1961, the Court disposed of this curious proposition. In a case coming from Ohio in which conviction clearly rested upon the use of evidence obtained in contravention to the injunction of the Fourth Amendment, the Supreme Court extended the federal rule to encompass all state jurisdictions. Henceforth any conviction in any jurisdiction in the United States which is based on illegally obtained evidence is in violation of the Constitution. *Mapp* v. *Ohio,* 81 S. Ct. 1684 (1961).

29. David Fellman, *The Defendant's Rights* (New York, 1958).

30. See Fellman's "The Constitutional Right to Counsel in Federal Courts," *Nebraska Law Review,* Vol. XXX, pp. 559 ff. (1951).

31. See *Moore* v. *Illinois,* 14 Howard 13 (1852) for an early examination of this problem.

32. See *Palko* v. *Connecticut,* 302 U.S. 319 (1937) where Justice Cardozo set out this rule in all its ambiguous splendor.

33. See *Herndon* v. *Lowry*, 301 U.S. 242 (1937). The Georgia
statute was ruled unconstitutional for "vagueness," though
it was no more vague (to take just one example) than
most conspiracy statutes. Clearly the Court had to get
Herndon off somehow and improvised an escape-hatch.
Could a statute get much more cloudy than the Smith Act
with its penalization of conspiracy to advocate and teach
the overthrow of the United States government by force
and violence? Compare Justice Jackson's brilliant dissent
in *Krulewitch* v. *United States*, 336 U.S. 440 (1949) in
which he eviscerated the doctrine of conspiracy with his
opinion in *Dennis* v. *United States*, 341 U.S. 494 (1951)
upholding the Smith Act. While this volume was in pro-
duction, the breach of the peace technique of avoiding
constitutional issues achieved nation-wide notoriety when
the "Freedom Riders" were arrested and sentenced in
Alabama for "disturbing the peace." Great care was exercised by the Alabama judiciary to assert for the record
that racial discrimination was in no way involved: the
"Riders" were convicted on a common law basis for making
a disturbance rather than for violating Alabama's "Jim
Crow" laws. Since these non-violent protests were not
planned as legal test cases (indeed, one announced purpose
was to "fill the jails"), those convicted did not raise the
appropriate legal issues; appeal thus becomes very difficult.
In one unrelated decision, however, the Court took the un-
precedented step of reversing a conviction in the Police
Court of Louisville, Kentucky, for "loitering and disorderly conduct." In a situation where the only basic
evidence for such conviction was a policeman's statement,
Justice Black stated, the Police Court's decision was not
founded on adequate evidence and constituted a denial of
Due Process. (It should be pointed out that Sam Thompson
was fortunate enough to be accompanied into the Police
Court by a crack civil liberties lawyer who raised the appropriate challenges at every point in the trial. This is an
excellent example of the role of the American Civil Liberties Union in defending the "rights" of the poverty-stricken:
if Mr. Louis Lusky, with the support of the Kentucky Civil
Liberties Union, had not gone into court with Thompson,
the latter's rights would have been nonexistent.) See
Thompson v. *Louisville*, 362 U.S. 200 (1960).

34. See Woodward, *Origins of the New South, op. cit.*

4. THE JUDICIARY AND THE DEMOCRATIC PROCESS

1. For a vivid description of the Court fight see James M. Burns, *Roosevelt: The Lion and the Fox* (New York, 1956).

2. The view from inside the Court can be found in Merlo J. Pusey, *Charles Evans Hughes* (New York, 1952), and Alpheus T. Mason, *Harlan Fiske Stone* (New York, 1956).

3. For the full development of this thesis see John P. Roche and Murray S. Stedman, Jr., *The Dynamics of Democratic Government* (New York, 1954).

4. For example, Charles Black, *The People and the Court* (New York, 1960) which turns "good" judicial review into a pillar of the democratic way of life.

5. An amazing, and in many ways pathetic, exercise of the iron fist. Polygamous Mormonism was suppressed, disclaimer oaths were required of voters, and the non-ecclesiastical property of the Mormon Church was seized by the government. The Supreme Court was unmoved; see *The Late Corporation of the Church of Jesus Christ of Latter-Day Saints* v. *United States,* 136 U.S. 1 (1890). The only adequate history of the Mormons is Ray B. West, Jr., *Kingdom of the Saints* (New York, 1957) which does not examine in any detail the legal basis of federal suppression. (Given the intended reach of the Fourteenth Amendment, Utah's territorial status does not invalidate the analogue.)

6. Some Republicans of long seniority, e.g., Styles Bridges, would have their choice between several committees. I have guessed at their probable decisions.

7. James O. Eastland, *The Supreme Court's "Modern Scientific Authorities" in the Segregation Cases,* pamphlet reprint of a speech delivered in the Senate, May 26, 1955 (Washington, 1955).

8. *Baltimore Contractors Inc.* v. *Carpenters' District Council of New Orleans,* 188 F. Supp. 382 (D.C., E.D. La., 1960).

The reference notes to basic sources, keyed to appropriate points in the manuscript, should serve the purposes of a bibliography. Cases have not been cited in the text, but are consolidated here in a Table of Cases. The reader who is interested further in pursuing any particular problem should develop the technique of "footnote hopping": beginning with the source cited, and the further sources listed there, he can move out into a large body of data. Leading Court decisions are thoroughly documented both with early cases and with secondary items of importance.

TABLE OF CASES

Adair v. U.S., 208 U.S. 161 (1908)
Allgeyer v. Louisiana, 165 U.S. 578 (1897)
American Insurance Co. v. Canter, 1 Pet. 511 (1828)
Barron v. Baltimore, 7 Pet. 243 (1833)
Brown v. Board of Education (School Segregation Cases), 347 U.S. 483 (1954)
In re Ah Fong (Twenty-one Chinese Prostitutes), 1 Fed. Cas. 213 (D. Cal., 1874)
Chisholm v. Georgia, 2 Dall. 419 (1793)
Civil Rights Cases, 109 U.S. 3 (1883)
Colegrove v. Green, 328 U.S. 549 (1946)
Coppage v. Kansas, 236 U.S. 1 (1915)